Complete Shotokan Karate
The Samurai Legacy and Modern Practice

D0838951

Complete Sh

Robin L. Rielly

otokan Karate

History, Philosophy, and Practice

Charles E. Tuttle Co., Inc.
Boston · Rutland, Vermont · Tokyo

First paperback edition published in 1998 by Tuttle Publishing, an imprint of Periplus Editions (HK) Ltd., with editorial offices at 153 Milk Street, Boston, Massachusetts 02109.

ISBN 0-8048-2108-9
Previously published as Karate Training
LCC# 84-051860

DISTRIBUTED BY:

USA	Japan	Southeast Asia
Tuttle Publishing	*Tuttle Shokai Ltd.*	*Berkeley Books Pte. Ltd.*
RR 1 Box 231-5	1-21-13, Seki	5 Little Road #08-01
North Clarendon,VT 05759	Tama-ku, Kawasaki-shi	Singapore 536983
Tel.: (802) 773-8930	Kanagawa-ken 214, Japan	Tel.: (65) 280-3320
Fax: (802) 773-6993	Tel.: (044) 833-0225	Fax: (65) 280-6290
	Fax: (044) 822-0413	

First edition
05 04 03 02 01 00 99 98   1 3 5 7 9 10 8 6 4 2
Printed in Singapore

Table of Contents

List of Illustrations

Foreword

by Teruyuki Okazaki
Instructor, Japan Karate Association
Chairman and Chief Instructor,
International Shotokan Karate Federation

I am pleased to be able to write this Foreword to Robin Rielly's book. Mr. Rielly received his early training in the martial arts in Japan and then became my student upon his return to the United States. His experiences in Japan gave him an interest in Japanese culture that has persisted to the present day. He belongs to a highly select group of American *karate-ka* who have been training for over twenty years in the martial arts. It is upon men such as him that we depend for passing on true karate to the Western world.

Since my arrival in America, I have actively tried to transmit to Americans the true spirit of karate-do and a real understanding of Japanese martial arts culture. Unfortunately, some of the concepts of the Japanese martial arts are difficult to transmit across cultural boundaries. Thus it is with great pleasure that I welcome the publication of this book, since it is the first such work to attempt to explain concepts that are not easily expressed in English. I wholeheartedly recommend it as essential reading for those who wish to understand not only Japanese karate, but the traditions and culture that have fostered it.

Preface

The writing of this book springs from two diverse interests on my part: one, an intellectual curiosity linked to my study of history and the other, a desire to explain more fully the philosophy of the arts that I have practiced for the last twenty-five years.

I have been more fortunate than many in that I have been able to study martial arts under some of the greatest contemporary masters. While in Japan I trained under Master Fumio Nagaoka, a top expert in Shin Kage-ryu jujutsu. I also benefited from the instruction given me by Eizo Onishi of the Koeikan School of Karate. Countless Japanese friends and other experts aided me in learning new techniques in both schools and left me with an unforgettable sense of camaraderie. Upon my return to the United States I was fortunate to become a student of Teruyuki Okazaki, one of the most famous Japan Karate Association masters and Chief Instructor of the International Shotokan Karate Federation. I have been his student since 1963. During the latter half of the 1960s, Master Okazaki was assisted in Philadelphia by two great Japanese national champions, Keinosuke Enoeda and Katsuya Kisaka. Their efforts on my behalf were significant, and I benefited greatly from their instruction. Yet I find that there is still much to learn and many techniques to be perfected.

In addition to providing technical and philosophical guidance for many years, Master Okazaki also read the manuscript and offered suggestions. Further help in that area was given by Glenn Rosenthal and my wife, Lucille, both of whom contributed greatly to the final product. My good friend Anthony Mirakian, foremost American expert on Goju-ryu karate, read the Okinawan section and provided valuable criticism in addition to his generous loan of many historical photographs.

Special thanks are due to Master Masatoshi Nakayama, Chief Instructor of the Japan Karate Association, for generously permitting the use of his calligraphy.

I am also indebted to John Kandes and Lucille Rielly for help with the photography. John Baatz, Thomas Finnerty, and Glenn Rosenthal consented to pose for the illustrations of the special sparring drills and the kata.

I owe a debt of gratitude to Professors Ardath W. Burks and Donald T. Roden of Rutgers University who, through the course of long discussions, gave me valuable insights into the nature of the samurai class and its ethos.

I must acknowledge a long-standing debt to two gentlemen who many years ago encouraged my academic attempts and have always been supportive. Professor Tadashi Kikuoka of the Institute of Far Eastern Studies, Seton Hall University, read the manuscript and offered valuable suggestions on the organization and content. Professor John B. Tsu provided early guidance that started me on the path to the study of history. To both I offer sincere thanks.

For their graciousness in granting me personal interviews, I would like to thank the following individuals: Masayuki Hisataki, Head Instructor of the Shorinji-ryu Kenkokan Karate Association; Roy Meyer, Regional Instructor for Gojukai Karate-Do U.S.A.; Anthony Mirakian, U.S. representative for Okinawan Meibukan Goju-ryu Karate; Teruyuki Okazaki, Chief Instructor of the International Shotokan Federation; Peter Urban, President of the United States of America Goju Association; and Gosei Yamaguchi, Chief Instructor of Gojukai Karate-Do, U.S.A.

Finally, I am indebted to the following individuals and institutions for the loan of illustrative materials listed below.
Anthony Mirakian: pp. 30, 34, 35, 37, 47
Philadelphia Museum of Art: p. 57 (Edmund L. Zalinsky Collection and gift of Mr. C. O. von Kienbusch); p. 58 (gift of Mrs. John D. Rockefeller); p. 63 (print purchased by subscription, supplemented by the Lola Downin Peck Fund); p. 77 (gift of Mrs. John D. Rockefeller)
University Museum, University of Pennsylvania: p. 25
West Coast Karate Association: p. 41

The work that follows is my sole responsibility and any shortcomings are my own.

ROBIN L. RIELLY

Toms River, N. J.

Introduction

Since the end of the Second World War there has been an increasing involvement on the part of Westerners in the study of the traditional Japanese martial arts of judo, kendo, aikido, and karate. The great increase in the practice of these arts has led to a significant interest in the culture of the country that generated them. Along with this interest has come a plethora of self-appointed experts who claim to have great insights into the nature of the warrior class in Japanese society. Using their "knowledge," they have passed themselves off as masters in the various combative arts and have led others to believe that they are subscribers to and propagators of some grand warrior ethos. Their actions have been significant, since they have quantitatively, if not qualitatively, given to the Occidental world a glimpse of the martial traditions of Japan. For the most part, these presentations have been incorrect, leading many Westerners to view martial arts practitioners as fakes. On the other hand, many who have little knowledge of Japan accept the assertions of these "experts" as correct and thus assist in the propagation of misconceptions. The end result is that there exists within the Western world today a considerable misunderstanding of Japanese martial arts and related aspects of Japanese society.

Misconceptions of foreign cultures are by no means unusual. Japanese have perceived Westerners incorrectly, and Westerners in turn have failed to understand the Japanese, Chinese, and Koreans. This problem, common throughout the history of man, is in large part attributable to a fascination for the unusual. Recently, those aspects of Japanese culture that have had the greatest appeal to Westerners have been those with the most exotic practices and philosophies. Karate, aikido, and Zen, for example, have proved of interest, not so much because of their intrinsic worth as for their value as curios. In many cases, the Westerners attracted to such exotic interests have in all likelihood been atypical representatives of their own cultures.

The beginnings of the distortions of the Japanese martial arts ethos came in the aftermath of World War II. At that time, many Americans were stationed in the Far East and came into contact with teachers of various combative systems. For many, the exposure was limited, and the brevity of their relationships left only a superficial impression of the true traditions of those arts. In other cases, individuals trained for a time with Japanese instructors who prostituted their art by selling black belt grades in order to make money. Some of these Americans left Japan with only a scant knowledge of the arts they were supposed to spread, and the resultant misunderstandings fostered by them are legion. Men with a year's training returned to the United States holding several grades of black belt rank with the permission of their Japanese instructors to represent them. Although the skill of these men was limited and their understanding of the philosophy of the art nonexistent, they were pressured by their former teachers and new students to teach a way of life that they had not mastered. In return for their allegiance, they were allowed to issue black belt grades sanctioned by the instructor in Japan or Okinawa, providing him with profitable registration and diploma fees. The new American "master" now had a vested interest, and even if philosophically his actions could not be condoned, they could certainly be justified from a monetary standpoint. In some cases the American instructor deluded himself, thereby giving rise to the worst kind of misrepresentation. As a true believer in his own philosophy of the martial arts, he was able to appear sincere and lead others down the same benighted path to misunderstanding. The student who encountered such an instructor could not help but be impressed by his manner, if not his technique. After all, the movements demonstrated by the American instructor were, if nothing else, exotic. His Japanese vocabulary, albeit limited, contained phrases and words that were designed to inspire the imagination and excite interest. Vast numbers of Americans searching for the unusual settled upon karate as a fulfilling endeavor, capable of providing the combination of physical and mental discipline that they sought.

At about the same time that these American instructors returned to the United States, the first Japanese instructors who had a full command of the martial arts also began to arrive. Some Americans who had trained in authentic schools in Japan sought out these Japanese instructors, resumed their training, and founded small clubs. This contingent became the core of true karate practitioners in the United States, those who followed the authentic teachings of the Japanese schools. The severity of the training and rigid discipline insured that their numbers were kept small, just as in Japan, where many train but few become high ranking belts. Even so, students of these new clubs found themselves training under the Japanese karate missionaries, such masters as Tsutomu Oshima, Hidetaka Nishiyama, Gosei Yamaguchi, Teruyuki Okazaki, Takayuki Mikami, Yoshiaki Ajari, and Fumio Demura.

By comparison, those schools run by the unqualified American instructors proliferated because of their exotic appearance and their appeal to the unusual. Training in them in many cases was inferior, and many of the students promoted to black belt would not have achieved such a rank in authentic karate clubs. The graduates of these schools in turn opened their own clubs and promoted students. Eventually, organizations were founded and had large numbers of people under their influence.

At first, the "pseudo-karate" practitioners wished to learn from those with real knowledge and were permitted to enter their tournaments. When they fared poorly, they attributed their losses to unfair judging and rejected any attempts to be indoctrinated into the correct practices. The classical schools continued to keep their standards and slowly grew, but their numbers, of course, were still not comparable to those of the less qualified. By the late 1960s many of the schools founded by the unqualified instructors had grown quite large and organized. They vied with the classical groups for Amateur Athletic Union recognition, considered then to be a forerunner to eventual Olympic competition. Whenever possible, they attempted to get further exposure through the media by showing the spectacular elements of the arts. Demonstrations of breaking ice and bricks, cutting an object placed upon a person's throat or stomach, and similar skills became quite popular, and the American public began to regard karate as something of a circus sideshow.

By the late 1970s the situation had reached the absurd. Men no older than twenty-five or thirty were appearing on televised sports shows and billing themselves as tenth-degree grand masters. Demonstrations of their alleged skill included catching bullets in their teeth and other acts probably never seen in Japan. The American public readily accepted their claims to black belt ranks, ranks in systems that they themselves had originated.

At about the same time, two of the most famous Japanese masters of the current century, Gogen Yamaguchi, the head of the Japanese Goju system, and Masatoshi Nakayama, the head of the prestigious Japan Karate Association, attained their tenth and ninth degree rankings, respectively, after lifetimes devoted to the study and propagation of true karate. Both of these men were in their sixties at the time of their achievements. In the United States, veteran instructors Nishiyama and Okazaki, men with over thirty years experience, finally earned eighth degrees. Although their efforts had produced many practitioners of authentic karate and their organizations were strong, they had not been truly appreciated by the public. The unqualified instructors had made their mark on the American audiences.

All the foregoing may seem to be rather pointless and the importance attached to the distinction made between the two groups of karate practitioners called into question. However, it must be remembered that the proliferation of those less-than-qualified instructors had led to misconceptions of Japanese martial arts by many Americans and, by extension, to great misunderstandings about Japanese culture. These distortions have been almost impossible for the classical combative groups to overcome. As a result, the author has long felt that some discussion of the traditions of the Japanese people and how those traditions are expressed in contemporary martial arts is necessary. Accordingly, the task at hand has several facets. First of all, it will be useful to survey the history of karate. In addition, an overview of the history of Japan during its military period will help to clarify the traditions that sprang from that time. The changes in these traditions and the adoption of these changes by the nation as a whole will also be discussed, including the influences that such mass adoption had on the practice of karate in Japan. A basic problem to be addressed here, however, is the difference between that which truly belongs to the past, the traditional, and that which mimics it, the "traditionalistic"; the modern-day *karate-ka* (karate practioner) who demonstrates his skill on the gymnasium floor is not the same as the Okinawan peasant who faced the Japanese samurai in the seventeenth century. Similarities in form exist, to be sure, but an examination of the history of these arts and the society that produced them may help to distinguish the traditional mode of thought from the contemporary traditionalistic trend.

Finally, a practical section including chapters on karate etiquette, kumite (training drills), and kata (set sequences of moves) is included.

PART ONE | **Karate and Tradition**

(Overleaf) *Do mu kyoku* (No limitation for life)
Calligraphy by Masatoshi Nakayama, presented to members of the East
Coast Karate Association.

Note: Oriental names are given surname first, except in the case
of Japanese living in modern times, whose surnames are given last.

Chinese place-names are rendered in the *pinyin* system of romanization; other Chinese words (personal names, traditional
martial arts terms, etc.) are given in their traditional spellings.

1

The History of Karate

At some point in man's ancient history he found it necessary to defend himself continuously from his fellows. This need for self-defense was usually a collective enterprise, as man did not live alone, but in extended families or small tribes. Eventually, these groups became large enough so that individual roles were defined. In primitive societies could be found men whose main duties were the making of weapons, hunting, or other related tasks. Throughout the feudal periods of history, wars between neighboring groups were carried on mainly by members of the aristocracy, and sometimes by peasants, who laid aside their farm implements and picked up weapons to defend their native soil.

As societies continued to grow, roles were further specialized to the extent that the economy was able to support a permanent military force. Classes of professional warriors, whose main task in life was to fight, came into existence. These were men who had the time and financial support that permitted the full-time practice of the methods of war and all its intricacies. These circumstances resulted in the development of the martial arts, the aim of whose training was to prepare men for war and to keep them in constant readiness should the need for their services arise. In different areas of the world this process took place at different times.

With the advent of firearms, the traditional martial arts began to decline in value. A conscripted soldier with a little training was capable of killing with one shot even the most heavily armored knight or the most skilled swordsman. The value placed on the arts of the sword, spear, and bow were denigrated. As this transition occurred, the continuous local warfare between neighbors began to lessen. In Japan, this began to take place when a unification process began in the seventeenth century.

The final step in the process (in Japan) that saw the decline of the warrior came with the Meiji Restoration of 1868, at which time the feudal system was abolished. Japan then saw the need to style her army along Western lines. Accordingly, the arts of the sword and spear took second place to the use of the rifle and artillery in the creation of a modern army. As Japan progressed and became involved at the turn of the century in a series of wars with other Asian countries and certain Western powers, the utilitarian function of those traditional arts declined. However, since they were a valuable part of the traditions of Japan and excellent builders of spiritual and physical strength, training in them was still encouraged. In order to derive the most benefit from their practice, newer types of contests had to be developed which would not see the death of the loser as a result. For example, the *shinai,* or bamboo sword, which had been used in schools of traditional sword fighting for centuries as a practice implement, became the principle weapon in the practice of kendo (sword fighting), while the live blade was reserved for practice in moves without an opponent (i.e., the kata; see Chapter 7). By wearing armor and using the *shinai,* schools could compete with one another and live to tell about it. Safe practice made it possible for the traditional arts, among them judo and karate, to develop into systems of physical education. In summary, the techniques of warfare had been transformed into means of physical conditioning, self-discipline, and even entertainment, that is, into sport.

In the remainder of this chapter, a general history of karate—and its development from martial art to sport—will be outlined. In subsequent chapters, the influence that the history and traditions of Japan had on this development will be examined in greater detail.

THE ORIGINS OF KARATE

Since man began his existence unarmed, systems of weaponless combat can be found throughout the world. In the Far East, these systems are very old and carry different names according to the geographical areas in which they are practiced, for example, *ch'uan-fa* in China, *taekwon-do* in Korea, and karate in Japan. For purposes of simplification the term "karate" is used herein to designate those Oriental combative arts whose main techniques involve striking an opponent with the hands or feet. In Asia this type of fighting has a long history. Among the unarmed fighting techniques, karate is perhaps the oldest form of pugilism.

The origins of the art are somewhat obscure, owing in part to the fact that it was frequently practiced in secret by groups vying for power. Since its history was not written, one has to rely on oral tradition, bits and pieces of information, and art works in order to present a complete picture.

Greek black-figured amphora depicting two boxers and their trainers. Courtesy of the University Museum, University of Pennsylvania.

According to legend, there existed in India a system of unarmed hand-and-foot fighting prior to 1000 B.C. Scant evidence substantiates its existence. It is known, however, that a warrior caste, the Kshatriya, dominated India before the advent of Buddhism and was in control until the rise of the Brahman caste. The Kshatriya were said to have practiced a bare-handed martial art known as *vajramushti,* a fighting technique that used the clenched fist as a weapon. There are numerous statues dating to the first century B.C. which depict temple guardians in poses similar to those used in fighting arts practiced later. It is these statues and the slight knowledge of the *vajramushti* which gives rise to the belief that karate may have originated in India. There is the possiblity, however, that the native Indian art may have been influenced by the Greeks. The conquests of Alexander the Great, who reached India in 327 B.C., may have led to the assimilation by the inhabitants of the Near East of certain fighting methods practiced in Greece.

The Greeks practiced a number of combative arts, among them a form of boxing which had long been a part of their culture. Perhaps the best evidence of the existence of such a fighting method in early times is the so-called "Boxers Vase" from Hagia Triada. Depicted on the sides of the vase are sports that have been interpreted as boxing and wrestling. The stances assumed by the figures closely resemble the *zenkutsu-dachi* (front stance) of modern Japanese karate. Two figures are depicted exchanging what seem to be counterpunches. In another scene one fighter has been thrown to the ground and his opponent stands over him ready to deliver a blow. The vase itself was produced on Crete, and other vases and bits of pottery with similar scenes have been found dating back to 1600 B.C.,[1] establishing the existence of karate-like fighting styles in the Western world at that time.

Various aspects of Greek boxing indicate that it more closely resembled Asian fighting than the modern Western style of boxing, although it had its own unique developments. One of the latter was the cestus, a device consisting of leather thongs and strips wrapped around the hand and forearm to increase striking power. Pottery fragments have been found that clearly show the use of these attachments. In a boxing contest, blows could be delivered with the open hand as well as with the clenched fist, and there was no prohibition against striking a fallen opponent. Weight classes were nonexistent in Greek boxing, just as in the practice of Asian karate. The heavyweight boxer, therefore, had the advantage.

One dissimilarity between Greek and Asian fighting was the emphasis of the former on blows to the head. In Asian systems, the body is considered to be the better target. This difference in emphasis might be explained by basic philosophic differences. The center of the Greek spirit was considered to be the head. Typical statues of Greek athletes depict a well-developed upper torso and a handsome face. The midsection is developed but is shown as a secondary feature. By contrast, statues of Asian temple guardians all show extremely well-developed and prominent abdomens. This may be attributed to the Oriental belief that the *seika tanden,* the "one point," located below the navel, is the center of the body.

Typical Greek boxing matches were not divided into rounds as in present-day boxing. Fights lasted until one fighter was knocked out or signaled defeat by raising his hand. (It is interesting to note that boxing may not have been practiced in Sparta, since one contestant would have to admit defeat, quite out of keeping with Spartan tradition.[2]) Since no ring was used, boxers could not corner an opponent and rely on infighting techniques. Therefore, the use of long range attacks, strong defensive positions, and the waiting out of the opponent came into play. This is very similar to a fight between karate enthusiasts, who traditionally wait to deliver the knockout blow. Indeed, a contest today between two high-ranked karate men may consist of several long periods of waiting followed by strong, vigorous attacks.

Roman boxing, incidentally, was less of a sport than a spectacle for popular amusement. The leaders of Rome felt that boxing was not an art that had practical military applications: far better if young warriors trained in the use of spear and sword. Boxing practice was left to the gladiators, who utilized a new, deadlier type of cestus, one with metal projections, that made the sport a bloody melee. As such, Roman boxing did not possess the skillful techniques or moral aspects of the Greek and Asian versions.

There existed in Greece another sport, known as the pankration, or "game of all powers," since at least 648 B.C., when it was instituted as an Olympic event.[3] This sport developed as a combination of earlier forms of Greek boxing and wrestling. In it, any technique except eye-gouging and biting was permitted (although some city-states may have allowed even this). Kicking was common, and statues exist that show practitioners competing what in modern karate would be called the front kick. Other techniques permitted were straight punches, jumping kicks, and throws similar to the *tomoe-nage,* or "circle throw," of judo, a move in which the thrower grasps the opponent's lapels and while falling backward, presses his foot in his adversary's stomach and throws him over his head. On some pottery fragments can be seen a front kick that has been caught with the defender moving in to sweep the supporting leg with a throw similar to judo's *o-uchi-gari* (inner-leg hook). Pankration contests were held under strict supervision, the referees using a long rod to strike the fighter who violated the rules. It was this form of empty-handed Greek art that most closely resembled Asian karate.

The pankration was not considered to be a "gentleman's sport" in the same way that Greek boxing was. In Plato's *Laws* (*c.* 350 B.C.) it may be observed that the "upright posture" was highly regarded.[4] Since the pankrationist had to leave his feet and assume the contrary poses in his fighting, Plato did not see the sport as beneficial to the correct development of young men. Indeed, he even criticized the use of such throwing and grappling techniques in the pankration by the fighters Antaeus and Cercyon as being useless in actual fighting and "unworthy of celebration." A young man should stand on his feet, not roll in the dust. This idea was a popular one and by the second century A.D. it was common to prohibit all wrestling techniques.

Some historians have discovered written evidence which, they claim, suggests that an early form of boxing existed in China. This ancient sport resembled more the pankration than the modern sport of boxing. E. Norman Gardiner mentions a boxing match between the marquis of Chin and the viscount of Chu in 631 B.C.[5] Apparently, the techniques used were not limited to punches, but included kicks and throws.

Still another method of training young men, also similar to karate, existed in ancient Greece. In *The Laws,* Plato described a dance called the pyrrhic as a mock battle in which the performer simulated the attitudes of attack and defense. The emphasis was on correct form and good posture. The dance was used as a means to train young men for fighting, but whether or not this Greek art had any influence on the fighting techniques of Asia is a matter for speculation. However, the descriptions of the pyrrhic by Plato might well be used to describe the traditional karate kata, or formal exercise. One thing that may be noted is that the pankration and the pyrrhic both antedate the Indian statues.

Although the discussion above indicates the existence of karate-like fighting arts in Greece, it is quite difficult to make any definite or substantial connection with present day martial arts in the Far East. Since the Greeks did maintain control of portions of the Near East that border on India, it is possible that elements of those two arts may have been introduced into India at that time. However, most historians seem content to trace the art of karate to the Indian *vajramushti* system. Even that investigation is hampered by a lack of evidence. Indeed, information about the Indian origins of karate is found only in legend and oral tradition.

FROM INDIA TO CHINA

India and China have a common border, so it is quite possible that the Indian *vajramushti* system was transmitted to China along with Buddhism. However, empty-handed fighting systems existed in China prior to the introduction of Buddhism, and any connection between Indian and Chinese fighting systems is difficult to prove. An examination of the legends of Chinese Buddhist monasteries, however, does seem to indicate a link between the Indian arts and the Chinese style of weaponless fighting known as *ch'uan-fa* (lit., fist way).

Perhaps the best-known branch of Buddhism in the Western world is the Zen sect. Called Dhyana in Sanskrit and Chan in Chinese, its teachings stress meditation as the way to achieve enlightenment. The founder of the Chan school in China is a fascinating, semi-legendary figure by the name of Bodhidharma (Daruma Taishi in Japanese). The myriad tales of his adventures and accomplishments in China are part of the folk legends of that country and make it difficult to distinguish fact from fiction.

Bodhidharma was born in India as a member of the Kshatriya caste. He was the third son of King Sugandha and was the twenty-eighth patriarch of Indian Buddhism. His real name was Bodhitara, which was later changed to Bodhidharma by his Dhyana master, Prajnatara. Bodhidharma remained in India studying under Prajnatara until the master died. It was at that point that he set out for China. Upon his arrival there Bodhidharma was invited to the court of Emperor Wu in Nanjing. The emperor had already developed a great interest in Buddhism and told Bodhidharma of the many good deeds he had performed. He described in detail the many Buddhist temples he had constructed, the Buddhist scriptures he had ordered his scholars to copy, and the favors he had granted to monks and nuns. Apparently, he felt that these material accomplishments would bring him merit. The emperor thereupon asked of the sage the extent of the merit due him. Bodhidharma immediately replied, "None at all." At that the emperor was surprised. He then asked his guest what the First Principle of Buddhism was and received the reply "nothingness." Somewhat annoyed with the monk, the emperor asked Bodhidharma who he thought he was. Bodhidharma said, "I do not know," and left. The emperor, after contemplating the monk's behavior for a while, sent a messenger after him to request his return. The envoy caught up with Bodhidharma just in time to see him cross the Yangzi River, supposedly standing upright on a reed. The legend then states that Bodhidharma traveled north from there to Henan Province where he took up residence at the Shaolin monastery in Sung Shan and began teaching the tenets of Chan Buddhism to the monks. According to another story, it was at that temple that Bodhidharma sat facing a wall for nine years in silent meditation, a feat which caused his legs to atrophy.

Still another tale, popular in martial arts circles today, concerns the connection between Bodhidharma and the founding of the form of *ch'uan-fa* of the Shaolin monastery. According to the legend, Bodhidharma was attempting to teach Chan to the monks at the Shaolin temple, an endeavor which subjected them to long periods of meditation. Many of them were in poor physical condition and the vigorous training of Bodhidharma left them on the verge of collapse. As a youth in India, Bodhidharma had learned the *vajra-mushti* fighting system. In order to strengthen the monks at Shaolin, he began teaching them this combat form. Soon the monks became known as the most formidable fighters in all of China. Supposedly, the system of physical exercise developed by him was the basis of the well-known Shaolin *ch'uan-fa* system, with succeeding masters adding to and improving upon original techniques until the more modern schools developed. (As mentioned previously, fighting forms existed in China before the introduction of Buddhism there. Thus, some Chinese martial arts exist which cannot trace their origins—historically or by legend—to Bodhidharma or the Shaolin temple.)[6]

The exercises that Bodhidharma taught his monks are said to have been written down in the *Hsien-Sui Ching* and *I-Chin Ching*. The former book has been lost, but the *I-Chin Ching* has supposedly been passed down through the ages. Some feel that none of the current versions is authentic; perhaps many of these texts were designed to perpetuate the myths about the monk. In spite of all the legends about him, however, it is generally accepted that he was in China sometime around A.D. 520 and did spread the Dhyana school of Buddhism there.

Chinese martial arts became increasingly popular during the Ming dynasty (1368–1644). However, with the rise to power of the Manchu, a Mongoloid people, many of the practitioners were forced to flee southward. They joined secret societies in order to help fight against the Manchu rulers and restore Chinese sovereignty. Opposition to the Manchu led to an increase in the number of boxing schools and secret Chinese societies, thus helping spread the arts throughout the country. Since the societies were instituted for the purposes of combat, it became necessary for the pugilists to become masters of Chinese weapons—the broad sword, the hooking sword, the plum-blossom sword, and the halberd—as well.

The customs of the boxers were not unlike those of the medieval Japanese fencing schools. The town boxing master taught selected students in private training sessions. Many students, in order to improve their proficiency, toured the country challenging these resident teachers. If the challenger lost, he would likely remain with his new master to study. If he won, the boxing teacher might be chased out of town and lose his school. The rules of combat specified that the challenger could decide whether weapons were to be used and, if so, what they would be. Therefore, a teacher had to be proficient with as many weapons as possible in order to protect his own interests. If

Examples of hard and soft systems: praying mantis and t'ai chi ch'uan being demonstrated by Kwan Tak-hing *(left)* and Cheng Man-ching *(right),* respectively.

the challenger was an unknown, the master might let him fight his senior students. This gave him time to observe the new opponent's technique and plan his strategy. If the students were defeated, the master would have to accept the challenge.

The proliferation of the boxing schools is obvious: there are over forty well-known systems extant in China today.[7] In the People's Republic of China, the general classification of martial arts, *ch'uan-fa,* has been changed to *wushu,* literally, "military arts." (Incidentally, the term common in the West for these arts, "kung-fu," is from a Cantonese word meaning "to be skillful at something"; it should not be applied to Chinese fighting systems, since its meaning is so general.) National contests are held in China, the arts being as popular as ever, particularly in light of the government's emphasis on physical fitness and the individual soldier. The warming of relations between the United States and China in the 1970s has made it possible for groups of Chinese martial artists to tour the United States and give demonstrations of their art.

No student of the martial arts today questions the idea that present-day karate systems were influenced by the Chinese, even though the possibility of some earlier Indian influence does exist. As one more point of historical background, the two main systems of Chinese martial arts, the exoteric, or hard, schools and the esoteric, or soft, schools are mentioned here. The exoteric schools, in which Shaolin *ch'uan-fa* is grouped, are generally considered to emphasize the building of strength in technique, speed, and agility in linear, angular movements—in short, the development of primarily physical techniques. The esoteric schools have tended to emphasize the building of strength in technique coupled with exercises that develop the mental concentration which allow the practitioner greater control over his body. Although one of the schools might be predominant according to location in China, most of present-day Japanese-Okinawan karate is oriented toward the exoteric systems.

OKINAWAN KARATE

Although native fighting systems existed in Okinawa and were known simply as *te* (lit., hand), there is general agreement among martial arts historians that there was significant Chinese influence that generated modifications to the art. When that influence began is debatable, with some writers asserting that it may have taken place as early as the Tang dynasty (A.D. 618–906).[8] Others claim that the first elements of a systematized fighting form were brought from China to Okinawa during the reign of Okinawan King Sho En (r. 1470–76),[9] but it is probable that the transmission began between these two extremes.

In 1372, King Satto of Okinawa established a tributary relationship with the Ming emperor in China. As a result, many Okinawans left their homes to reside in China as part of the Okinawan mission, and many Chinese went to Okinawa with the Chinese delegation. These Okinawans brought back elements of Chinese fighting arts and combined them with the existing system of Okinawan unarmed combat, producing *tode* (lit., Tang hands), a new, more organized system of self-defense. To that time, the Okinawan *te* had been characterized by the use of the clenched fist. However, the Chinese influence that produced the new art of *tode* saw the introduction of more varied techniques. One influence, from Taiwan, was the use of the spearhand *(nukite)*; another, the open-hand *(kaishu)* techniques borrowed from Chinese *ch'uan-fa*. Kicking techniques in the Okinawan arts were largely the result of influences from southern Chinese systems. Most authorities agree that later karate developed as a result of influences from *ch'uan-fa* and *tode*.

In 1393 a group of Chinese craftsmen and administrators were sent to Okinawa by Emperor Hung Wu to show support for the regime of King Satto and to demonstrate to the Okinawans the superiority of Chinese administrative and shipbuilding methods. The settlement that they founded near Naha became known as the "thirty-six families," a term used at that time to designate a large group of people. Okinawan legends credit the members of this group with the spread of *ch'uan-fa*. Meitoku Yagi, current master of the Goju-ryu school, traces his ancestry to a Chinese *ch'uan-fa* master who was a member of one of those families.

Okinawa was unified under King Sho Hashi in 1429. Sea trade was encouraged, leading to the development of two great ports, Shuri and Naha. In succeeding years, Okinawans gained fairly extensive knowledge of Southeast Asian forms of combat as a result of their trade in that part of the world. Later, under King Sho Shin (r. 1477–1526), the first prohibition of weapons took place.

In 1609 the Satsuma clan of southern Kyushu, Japan, led by Shimazu Iehisa, took control of Okinawa. Shimazu instituted firm control over the populace, placing many restrictions on the natives, including a continuing ban on weapons. All arms found were confiscated and the owners severely punished. The Okinawans were resentful and conflicts arose between them and their Japanese rulers, resulting in the practice of weaponless fighting in earnest. In addition, the severe pressure placed on the Okinawans by the Japanese forced the diverse schools to cooperate with each other, which led to an improvement in technique. Thus, the imported *ch'uan-fa* was able to further influence the native forms of the martial arts. The art that arose as a result of this unification was referred to simply as *te,* a return to the original terminology of the region.

Since the new art had to be learned in secret, little was written about it. In time, the term was prefixed by the name of the town in which it was practiced. Subsequently, three major schools developed: Shuri-te, Tomari-te, and Naha-te. Shuri-te, an exoteric system, emphasized speed and combined techniques with rational (practical) movements. Naha-te combined the Chinese hard and soft techniques, using rational, dynamic movements and emphasizing breathing, flexibility, and strength. Tomari-te has been described as containing elements of both Naha-te and Shuri-te systems, with added stress on speed and agility. A twentieth-century karate master, Gichin Funakoshi, would claim that Tomari-te was more suitable for men of slight build, as it matched their fighting style, while the Naha-te was more suited for self-defense, but lacked mobility.[10] In time, Shuri-te and Tomari-te became known as the Shorin style and Naha-te as the Shorei style. Because it was practiced in secret, *te* took on a certain exotic air and became extremely violent, having the immediate extinction of an opponent as its chief goal.

Kanryo Higaonna

Perhaps the greatest master of Naha-te in the history of Okinawan karate was Kanryo Higaonna (1851–1915). Higaonna, known as Kensei (lit., fist saint), studied in Fuzhou, China, for over twenty years under the *ch'uan-fa* master Liu Liu-ko. In addition, he was one of the top students of the famous Shuri-te master Sokon Matsumura.

The end of Satsuma rule in 1872 led to an intense rivalry between the Shuri, Naha, and Tomari schools, since they had no common enemy left to fight. This further resulted in open quarrels and a bad reputation for the art in general. However, in 1902 karate finally surfaced from the depths of secrecy. The Okinawans, recognizing its valuable character-building aspects, introduced it as a part of the physical education curriculum of the First Middle School of Okinawa upon the suggestion of Shintaro Ogawa, Commissioner of Schools for Kagoshima Prefecture.[11] (Okinawa was officially a part of Japan by then.) The first instructor was Anko Itosu. Shortly thereafter, a number of men became well known as karate masters. Among them were Gichin Funakoshi, Chotoku Kyan, Kenwa Mabuni, Choki Motobu, Uden Yabu, Chojo Ogusuku, Chojun Miyagi, Chomo Hanashiro, Kentsu Yabu, Juhatsu Kiyoda, and Ankichi Arakaki. Many of them were responsible for the later introduction of karate systems into Japan.

Today there are five major systems of karate practiced on Okinawa: Uechi-ryu and Goju-ryu, which are descended from Naha-te; and Shorin-ryu, which is divided into Matsubayashi-ryu, Kobayashi-ryu, and Shorin-ryu. The three subgroups of Shorin-ryu are descendents of Shuri-te. All the styles are organized into the All-Okinawan Karate-Do Association, the official body governing the martial arts on Okinawa.

Uechi-ryu is the Okinawan name for the Chinese system called Pon-gai-noon. It was founded by Kanbun Uechi, who went to China in 1901 to study *ch'uan-fa*. He returned years later and founded his school on Okinawa. At this time, his son, Kan'ei Uechi, is the head of the system of Uechi-ryu

Chojun Miyagi

on Okinawa and has eight schools under his control. He has also served as one of the directors of the All-Okinawan Karate-Do Association.

Goju-ryu (lit., hard-soft style) was founded as a separate system by the late Chojun Miyagi in the 1920s. Born in Naha City, Okinawa, in 1888, Miyagi trained in the Naha-te school under Kanryo Higaonna from 1902 to 1915. He then sailed to Fuzhou and studied there until 1917 in such Chinese styles as Pa-kua Hsing-i, Mi Tsung-i, and "tiger-crane" Shaolin. Master Miyagi spent his entire life contributing to the improvement and proliferation of karate-do. He died in 1953 on Okinawa, leaving the Goju school to Meitoku Yagi, his highest-ranked disciple. Yagi inherited Miyagi's belt on the tenth anniversary of the master's death.

One of the Shorin-ryu schools, the Matsubayashi-ryu, was founded in 1947 by Shoshin Nagamine, a contemporary karate master who studied his art under Ankichi Arakaki, Chotoku Kyan, and Choki Motobu. The Kobayashi-ryu branch of Shorin-ryu was founded by Choshin Chibana, while the third branch, Shorin-ryu, dates back to Sokon Matsumura, a famous Shuri-te master.

JAPANESE KARATE

Karate had been practiced in many countries of the Orient since early times, but did not receive a formal introduction to the Japanese public until 1922, when Okinawan karate master Gichin Funakoshi gave a demonstration in Japan. Funakoshi, born in Shuri in 1868, had studied under Shuri-te masters Anko Itosu and Yasutsune Azato. An elementary school teacher by occupation, Funakoshi was invited by the Central Secretariat of Physical Education to go to Tokyo to demonstrate karate at the National Athletic Championships. The founder of Kodokan judo, Jigoro Kano, was so impressed that he invited Funakoshi to stay and teach karate at the Kodokan Judo

Gichin Funakoshi

Hall. Funakoshi accepted the invitation and also began to give instruction at the Butokukai Military Arts College in Kyoto and at Keio University in Tokyo. In the early 1930s he established his own school in Tokyo.

Funakoshi practiced calligraphy and signed his work "Shoto," his pen name. Hence, the school where he taught came to be known as Shotokan, "Shoto's School," and the system as Shotokan-ryu. Master Funakoshi never labeled his system as such; the name was adopted by students and outsiders. Rather than teaching a pure system of karate, he combined the teachings of masters Azato and Itosu (of the Shuri-te/Shorin lineage) with elements of the Shorei systems so that the Shotokan-ryu has ended up containing techniques and kata of the two major styles. As a result, modern day Shotokan includes the breathing kata common to the Shorei school and also the lighter, more flexible movements of the Shorin school.

Chojun Miyagi, the founder of Goju-ryu of the Naha-te line, began teaching karate at Kyoto Imperial University in 1928. (He later became coach of the karate department of Kansai University in Osaka.) The Goju-ryu line was further perpetuated in Japan by Gogen Yamaguchi, one of Miyagi's early students, who formed a karate club at Ritsumeikan University (Kyoto) in 1930. Yamaguchi made a significant contribution to Japanese karate by devising a form of free-style sparring that had not existed in the traditional Okinawan Goju system. In 1935 he organized the All-Japan Gojukai Karate-Do Association and became its chief instructor. Sent to Manchuria in 1939 as an intelligence officer, he was captured by the Russians. In 1947 he was repatriated to Japan and continued performing his responsibilities at his Association. A survey in 1967 found some 300,000 people practicing karate under Yamaguchi's system.

The year 1930 saw another Okinawan, Kenwa Mabuni, in Japan. Mabuni, who had studied under both Anko Itosu and Kanryo Higaonna, founded a new system, the Shito-ryu, by combining the techniques of his teachers with

Kenwa Mabuni disarming a sword-wielding attacker.

other systems. He derived the name "Shito" by joining alternate pronunciations of the Chinese characters for "Ito" and "Higa," from the names of his two teachers. Today Shito-ryu is widely practiced in Japan, under the auspices of the All-Japan Karate Federation.

Hironori Otsuka began studying with Gichin Funakoshi at the Tokyo Shotokan in 1926. In 1935 he formed his own school, the Wado-ryu, or "way of peace" style, combining Okinawan karate with elements of traditional Japanese martial arts. Until his death in 1982, he headed the Japan Karate-Do Federation and had several hundred clubs under his authority.

In about 1935, one of Kenwa Mabuni's students of Shito-ryu, Masaru Sawayama, broke away from his master and founded kempo, a combination of karate, judo, and boxing in which the players wear protective equipment. Kempo is organized under the All-Japan Kempo Federation. The founding of kempo gave Japan a total of four main styles of karate—Shotokan-ryu, Goju-ryu, Shito-ryu, and Wado-ryu—and one of kempo.

It might be noted that although Sawayama called his new style "kempo," this was not the first such use of the name in Japan. The Japanese had a long interest in things Chinese, and virtually all fistic arts with any Chinese influence were known by that name. One art that claimed Chinese influence was established in Japan in 1930 and labeled "Shorinji kempo" by its founder, Taizen Takemori. Organizations dedicated to the study of Shorinji kempo were begun after World War II, one of which is the All-Japan Shorinji-ryu Kenkokan Karate Federation, founded by Masahara Hisataka. (Note that this "Shorinji" has no relationship to the Shorin-ryu of Okinawan karate.)

A ban placed on the martial arts of Japan in 1945 by the American occupation forces was rescinded about two years later. The arts began to flourish again, and by 1948 Japanese karate men, mostly students of Gichin Funakoshi, had organized the Japan Karate Association to honor the master. Funakoshi served as honorary chief instructor and his senior student, Isao Obata of Keio University, was named chairman. The karate clubs of Keio, Hosei, Waseda, and Takushoku universities formed the backbone of the organization. Masatoshi Nakayama, a graduate of Takushoku University who had studied Chinese fighting arts in Beijing, was appointed chief instructor. (At the time of this writing, Nakayama is still serving in this capacity at the Japan Karate Association. At the age of 69, he holds the 9th dan rank.)

The newly founded Japan Karate Association was not, however, without its troubles, mostly based upon old college rivalries. Many of the college alumni clubs, including the Keio University group, quit. Even amid these difficulties, though, the Japanese Ministry of Education sanctioned the Japan Karate Association as an educational institution in 1957. That year, the Association held the first All-Japan Karate Championships, which have since become an annual event.

An important school of karate separate from the "big four" schools mentioned so far is the Kyokushinkai karate system, organized by Masutatsu Oyama in 1957. Oyama, a Korean whose real name is Yong I-choi, was born near Gunsan, Korea, in 1922. In 1938 he left home for Japan, where he studied Shotokan karate under Gichin Funakoshi. He then switched to Gojuryu under Neichu Sou. At this time he heads the Kyokushinkai karate system, which has branches throughout the world.

Finally, in 1965 the Federation of All-Japan Karate-Do Organizations (FAJKO) was formed, uniting most of the major schools of karate in Japan, including the "big four." Representatives for the four major schools were Hironori Otsuka (Wado), Gogen Yamaguchi (Goju), Ken'ei Mabuni (Shito), and Masatoshi Nakayama (Shotokan). Ryoichi Sasagawa was made president of the Federation.

For the most part, karate systems practiced in Japan contain forms that are predominantly Okinawan in origin, although some evidence of Chinese influence can be found. The Japanese, however, have managed to develop a unique system, owing in large part to changes wrought over the past several decades. Those changes have been directly influenced by traditional arts such as kendo and judo.

Masatoshi Nakayama training a class in Philadelphia on one of his many visits to the United States.

KARATE: THE NAME CHANGES

Sometime in the late 1800s the pronunciation "karate" 唐手 (lit., Tang hand) came into use to designate the arts that had previously been called *tode* (also written with the characters 唐手), and even earlier, simply *te* 手. This took place on Okinawa and reflected the respect that the Okinawans had for China, since the character 唐 stood for the Tang dynasty. In 1904, Chomo Hanagi departed from the old way of writing "karate" when he used the character 空 *kara* in place of 唐 *kara* in his book *Karate Soshu Hen,* the first work in which this character was used in reference to the art. It reflected the growing spirit of Japanese nationalism and the rejection of things Chinese. For those who had long been practicing the art, however, it was still called *te,* or in some cases *bushi-no-te* 武士の手 (lit., warrior's hand).

In the 1920s Gichin Funakoshi suggested that the new way of writing of the term "karate" 空手 (lit., empty hand) was perhaps more appropriate, since the art seemed Okinawan and Japanese rather than Chinese. In addition, Funakoshi felt that the art should be labeled "empty hand," since no weapons were used. Perhaps a more important point, however, was that he felt that there was a common link between the traditional Zen-oriented martial arts of Japan and the art that he practiced (see p. 64). Thus the *kara* he spoke of described a void that approximated the concept of nothingness so greatly discussed by Buddhists. If the mind could be emptied of all earthly desires as the Buddhists held, then perfection in the art could be reached. This was the teaching of Zen masters who were adept at the arts of war in feudal Japan. The changing of the character used to write the word "karate" showed that the traditional Okinawan combat system was becoming Japanized and was taking on the same traditions as the classical arts of the sword and the bow.

THE TRANSMISSION OF KARATE TO THE UNITED STATES

Over a decade ago, when I was researching my first book, *The History of American Karate*,[12] I found that there were some complications present in the identification of the first teacher of karate in the United States. Numerous questionnaires were therefore sent to all known schools of karate in the United States, well over 500 at that time. The survey requested information about the origins of each club and the background of its instructor. Unfortunately, many falsified surveys were returned: it seemed that many wished to claim the title "Father of American Karate." At that time I had to make some judgments as to the authenticity of the responses and the qualifications of the claimants. My opinion is the same now as it was then, that the current karate movement in the United States began in 1955 with Tsutomu Oshima. He has continued to contribute to the growth of American karate since that time.

The following questions had been asked in the survey:

1. What was the date that the instructor began teaching in the United States?

2. Was the instructor seriously involved in the instruction of martial arts or was it only an occasional activity?

3. Were the results of the instruction such that the program of instruction might be termed successful? That is, did he in fact produce advanced students and instructors who were then able to carry on the traditions and activities associated with the art?

4. What were the qualifications of the instructor? Was he well trained in the arts himself and qualified to pass them on?

5. Was the karate he taught recognized as authentic?

Oshima began his club in 1955 at the Konko Shinto Church in Los Angeles. A graduate of Waseda University in 1953, he had studied Shotokan karate under Gichin Funakoshi for six years and also with Funakoshi's senior student at that time, Shigeru Egami. This point answers the fourth and fifth questions favorably, since he had received lengthy instruction from a recognized master of a traditional art and was thus exceptionally well qualified to pass his knowledge on to others. By contrast, many other claimants studied unknown or minor systems under less than favorable conditions. In 1956 Oshima formed the South California Karate Association and has been its

Hidetaka Nishiyama refereeing a contest at the 1967 All-America Karate Championships, Los Angeles.

leader since that time. During the past two and a half decades he has trained many instructors and created a nationwide federation, Shotokan Karate of America. Since he has devoted his life to the instruction of the classical art of karate, it stands to reason that he has fulfilled the criteria in points 2 and 3.

A number of the individuals who responded to the survey claimed to have developed their own style of karate, based on one or two years of experience in the Far East. However, it has to be assumed that their mastery of the art was not complete after so short a training period, thereby contradicting their claim to the title.

Other Shotokan instructors took Oshima's place when he left California for a visit home. It became necessary for him to remain in Japan, so he arranged to have Hidetaka Nishiyama, a student of Master Funakoshi's at Takushoku University, come to Los Angeles to instruct in his place. When Oshima returned to the United States in 1963 to resume leadership of the South California Karate Association, Nishiyama continued to work with his newly founded All-America Karate Federation (AAKF), the American branch of the Japan Karate Association.

Another student of Gichin Funakoshi's (and also of Master Funakoshi's successor, Masatoshi Nakayama) who came to the United States was Teruyuki Okazaki. Okazaki began teaching in a small karate club in Philadelphia in 1961. The next year he founded the East Coast Karate Association, a branch of Nishiyama's All-America Karate Federation. Early in 1965, a group of black-belt holders from Okazaki's club in Philadelphia broke away and formed their own group, known as the Delaware Valley Karate Association; it later became affiliated with Oshima's Shotokan group. Another breakaway took place in recent years when Okazaki and a number of others left Nishiyama's group, forming the International Shotokan Karate Federation. This group, along with Nishiyama's, is recognized by the Japan Karate

Table 1
GENEOLOGY OF SHOTOKAN-RYU

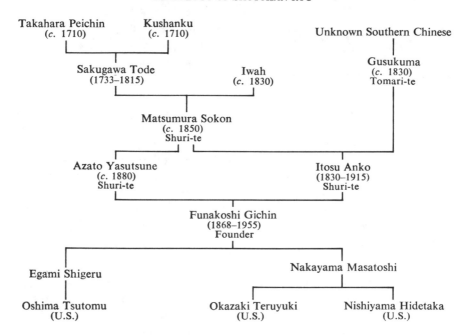

Note: In the four geneological tables all Oriental names are given surname first.

Association, thus giving the JKA two representative organizations in the United States.

The next school of Japanese karate to begin being taught in the United States, in 1960, was Goju-ryu. This took place when Peter Urban opened a school in Union City, New Jersey. Urban had studied the system while he was stationed in Japan, first under Richard Kim, and later under Masters Gogen Yamaguchi and Masutatsu Oyama, from 1953 to 1959. Urban represented the Japanese Goju system on the East coast of the United States until his resignation in 1966, when he founded his own group.

The Japanese felt that more could be done with Goju-ryu in the United

Table 2

GENEOLOGY OF GOJU-RYU

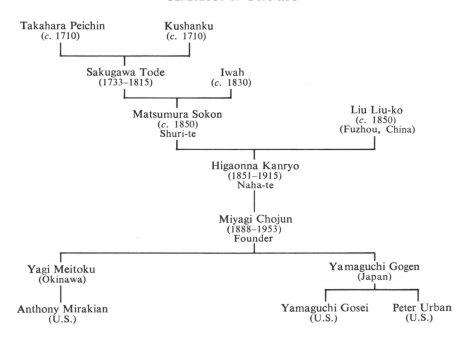

States; they thought that the language barrier may have hindered the accurate transmission of the art. Accordingly, Master Yamaguchi decided to send his sons to the United States to teach. In 1963 Gosen Yamaguchi, the second son, enrolled in San Francisco State College. He founded a club there and opened a private school off campus in San Francisco. In 1964 his elder brother, Gosei, arrived in San Francisco and began teaching. He soon founded the Gojukai Karate-Do U.S.A. as America's official branch of the International Karate-Do Gojukai. Goshi Yamaguchi, the third son, came to the United States to teach in Kansas City in 1965. The Gojukai group participated with the All-America Karate Federation and the U.S.Wadokai Federation in presenting several All-America Karate Tournaments in the 1960s.

Table 3
GENEOLOGY OF WADO-RYU

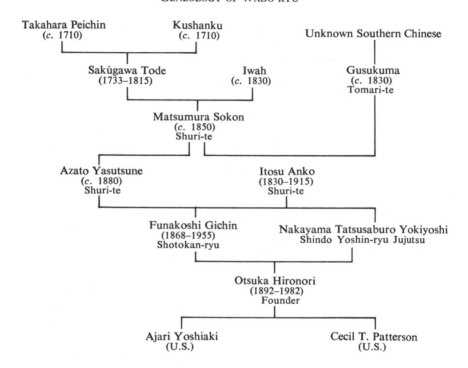

Takahara Peichin (c. 1710)
Kushanku (c. 1710)
Unknown Southern Chinese

Sakûgawa Tode (1733–1815)
Iwah (c. 1830)
Gusukuma (c. 1830) Tomari-te

Matsumura Sokon (c. 1850) Shuri-te

Azato Yasutsune (c. 1880) Shuri-te
Itosu Anko (1830–1915) Shuri-te

Funakoshi Gichin (1868–1955) Shotokan-ryu
Nakayama Tatsusaburo Yokiyoshi Shindo Yoshin-ryu Jujutsu

Otsuka Hironori (1892–1982) Founder

Ajari Yoshiaki (U.S.)
Cecil T. Patterson (U.S.)

Masutatsu Oyama's Kyokushinkai first came to the United States in November 1961, at which time the leader gave a demonstration at the North American Championships in Madison Square Garden, New York City. Since that initial demonstration, a number of Americans have become affiliated with the system and have helped its development. Two of Oyama's senior students from Japan, Tadashi Nakamura and Shigeru Oyama, began teaching in New York in the late 1960s and the group has continued to grow since then.

The main organization in the United States for the style of Japanese karate known as Wado-ryu is the Wadokai Karate-Do Federation. It was founded on April, 7, 1963, by Yoshiaki Ajari, a student of the founder of Wado-ryu,

Table 4
GENEOLOGY OF SHITO-RYU

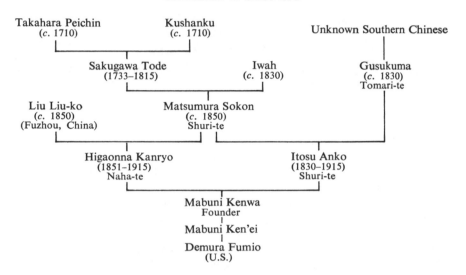

Takahara Peichin
(c. 1710)

Kushanku
(c. 1710)

Unknown Southern Chinese

Sakugawa Tode
(1733–1815)

Iwah
(c. 1830)

Gusukuma
(c. 1830)
Tomari-te

Liu Liu-ko
(c. 1850)
(Fuzhou, China)

Matsumura Sokon
(c. 1850)
Shuri-te

Higaonna Kanryo
(1851–1915)
Naha-te

Itosu Anko
(1830–1915)
Shuri-te

Mabuni Kenwa
Founder

Mabuni Ken'ei

Demura Fumio
(U.S.)

Hironori Otsuka. Ajari had also studied Goju-ryu style karate under Gogen Yamaguchi and Shozo Ujita. At the time of his arrival in America, he held the sixth-degree black belt. Since its founding, the Wadokai has spread throughout the San Franscisco Bay area and includes a student club at the University of California Berkeley campus. In 1967, Hidetaka Abe, a graduate of Meiji University, came to the United States to assist Ajari. He was followed shortly thereafter by Hironji Nagaoka, a third-degree black belt. These men concentrated their efforts on the West coast, with the result that this area became the stronghold for the Wadokai in the United States. Ajari believes that the style of karate he learned originally has changed since its introduction to America, although it still resembles closely the original system as taught in Japan. Since he had also studied Goju-ryu, he added some training methods and techniques from that style. Along with the Gojukai and the AAKF, Ajari cooperated with the running of the All-America Karate Championships in the 1960s.

The other of Japan's "big four" schools, Shito-ryu, came to the United

Shito-ryu master Fumio Demura *(right)* demonstrating his kicking technique.

States with Fumio Demura, a former student of Ken'ei Mabuni (the son of the founder of that school). Demura began teaching at Dan Ivan's school in Santa Ana, California in 1966. Since that time he has founded his own organization for the furtherance of his style in the United States. Other Shito-ryu organizations exist in America; among them are the Shukokai of New Jersey, and one begun by Julius Thiry in Seattle, Washington, in 1966.

There are two styles of kempo practiced in the United States today: Shorinji kempo and the system of the All-Japan Kempo Federation. The schools of the latter were founded in the West coast by Goki Kinnya in 1961, and were organized into the American-Nippon Kempo Federation. Master Kinnya remained in California until 1967, when he returned to Japan. He left a number of students qualified to pass on the art.

Shorinji kempo was brought to the United States in 1963 by Masayuki Hisataka, the son of the founder of one such system and a graduate of Nihon University. Hisataka founded the Shorinji-ryu Kenkokan Karate Federation of the United States. He taught in New York City from 1963 to 1967 and then left for Canada. In his absence a number of his senior students have continued his work.

The organizations of the "big four" karate schools are not limited to the United States, but are worldwide in scope. Grades awarded are generally held in high esteem. In addition to these, there are many other traditional and legitimate systems practiced in Japan today. Among these are Shudokan, Koeikan, Chito-ryu, and Kinto-ryu. A number of them have produced non-Japanese black belts who have returned to their homes to teach. In some cases Japanese instructors from these organizations have left their country to assist in the spread of their art.

Anthony Mirakian *(far left)* leading his students in performing a kata.

Besides the transmission of Japanese karate to the United States, there has been some direct influence from Okinawa itself due to the presence of American servicemen there in the decades following World War II. One such serviceman was George Mattson of Massachusetts, who studied Uechi-ryu karate under Ryuko Tomoyose in the late 1950s. Mattson was the first American to receive a black belt in that style. Upon his return to Massachusetts, he opened the first Uechi-ryu school in America. Since that time he has taught a number of students who have branched out in the Boston area to open their own schools.

Shorin-ryu karate at present has no major, nationwide organization in the United States. There are, however, a number of unaffiliated schools teaching the art. The Kobayashi branch is represented in this country by Seikichi Iha, Kina Santos, and Kensai Taba, all high-ranking experts in the system. They have toured the country a number of times giving demonstrations of the art. Sid Campbell, a serviceman who studied in the Far East, founded the Shorin-ryu Karate-Do Club in Oakland, California in 1967. He originally trained under Shugoro Nakazato, a high-ranked master. Various other Americans have received training from Okinawan Shorin-ryu masters and have returned to spread the art. Some of these are James Kennedy and Rowland Cadaret (students of Soken Hohan and Fusei Kise); Richard Delling, Sam Pearson, and Roland Albarado (students of Eiso Shimabuku); and James Wax, Frank Grant, and Tommy Morita (students of Shoshin Nagamine).

The pioneer of Okinawan Goju-ryu in the United States is Anthony Mirakian, who founded the Okinawan Karate-Do Academy in Watertown, Massachusetts in 1960. In the 1950s Mirakian was stationed on Okinawa as a member of the U.S. Air Force. His first teacher was Seikichi Toguchi, president of the Shoreikan School of Goju Karate. He also studied under Ryu-ritsu Arakaki and later received his highest training under the present head of the Goju system, Master Meitoku Yagi, president of the Meibukan School of Goju-ryu. Mirakian is the only karate student from the United States to have received a black belt from Master Yagi. Mirakian is now the North American representative for Meibukan Goju-ryu karate-do, and is the foremost authority in the United States on the technical, historical, and philosophical concepts of Okinawan Goju-ryu karate.

In addition to the main schools of Okinawan karate already mentioned, there are others that exist in the United States. One very popular style is the Isshin-ryu system, founded by Tatsuo Shimabuku after World War II. Shimabuku had originally trained in Shorin-ryu under Chotoku Kyan and Choki Motobu, but synthesized their teachings and formed a new style. The first man to introduce Isshin-ryu to the United States was Don Nagel in 1957. He opened a school in Jacksonville, North Carolina, and later moved his school to Jersey City, New Jersey. Since that time he has taught a number of students who have branched out and formed schools of their own, in some cases altering the style that Nagel taught. The two main vehicles for Isshin-ryu in the United States are the American-Okinawan Karate Association, headed by Steve Armstrong, and the International Isshin-ryu Karate Association, run by Harold Long. Another high-ranking Isshin-ryu practitioner is Harold Michum of Indiana, who is independent of the main organizations.

Thus has the art of karate-do developed, its transition continuing even in the present day. In the past three decades it has been organized as a sport and now commands a following large enough for inclusion in the Olympic Games. Olympic competition, however, is not the goal of most practitioners. In a dojo, or training hall, may be found those whose main goals more closely follow the philosophy of the earlier years. Training for physical fitness and self-discipline seems to be the major objective of most serious practitioners today. The emphasis on self-discipline is amplified to the point where perfection of technique has become the paramount goal of the trainee. As such, karate training has almost become a philosophy that carries dedication to perfection into other areas of the karate practitioner's life. When this stage has been reached, one can truly be considered to be practicing karate as a *do,* or way of life.

2

The Samurai and His Ethos

The long history of the Japanese people is little known to the average reader; however, the warrior class that ruled Japan for seven centuries, the samurai, is more familiar to Westerners. What many readers do not recognize is the effect that the samurai had on Japanese society and culture, including the practice of modern-day martial arts. Since within the Japanese systems of karate certain centuries-old cultural traits are evident, it will be interesting to trace the development of the Japanese martial ethos through the rise and development of the samurai class, the original bearer of these traits.

The warrior class began to rise in the eighth century, and within the next four hundred years developed from a group of armed guards and soldiers into a class that ruled Japan through its *bakufu,* or military government. Until the nineteenth century the samurai held the uppermost position in the Japanese class structure. They developed a value system known as bushido, which became the heritage of the Japanese nation as it entered the twentieth century. What bushido was and how it developed is important to the understanding of Japanese karate and other martial arts, since it was, and is, an integral part of the Japanese character and is evident in Japanese karate-do. Other influences, most notably that of Zen, also played an important role in the development of the samurai ethos and Japanese martial arts.

THE ORIGINS OF THE SAMURAI

Prior to the seventh century A.D. Japan was ruled by a warrior aristocracy organized in extended clans. Mounted on horseback, these warrior-aristocrats controlled local sections of the country; the ties that bound the various leaders together were loose. Toward the end of the seventh century, under Empress Jito, the system began to change. Chinese influence was great, the empress being a great admirer of the social system of the Tang dynasty. She was responsible for a division of the society into civil and military with her appointments of officials to military posts. Under her direction a war office was organized and various high-ranking officers were commissioned. In addition, infantry and cavalry units were set up in each district.

At that time, the class known now as the samurai did not exist. No hereditary designation automatically placed a child in the vocation of warrior. Commoners were given tax exemptions to serve in the armed forces and all citizens were able to carry arms. Eventually, however, strong and influential families managed to usurp the power of the state. These families gained control of the military posts which had formerly been under the administration of the sovereign. To investigate the origins of these families and how they developed into a military class and gained such power requires some study of the economic system of that time.

The beginnings of the military class can be traced to the manorial system of the Nara period of Japan's history (710–84), but some earlier background should be mentioned first. In 645, what is known as the Taika Reform had taken place, in which the central government (that of the emperor) claimed control of all rice land, with a view to allotting such land to the people in general. To appease the former owners of large tracts of land, the government allowed them to keep control of their holdings, and conferred rank and privilege upon them. Unfortunately, the still powerful "owners" were exempt from heavy tax burdens, while the ordinary, new tract holders were not. The latter often donated their plots to the former, effectively exempting themselves from taxes, but still working the land and paying a fee to the new landholder.

With the population steadily increasing, the central government in 723 decreed that three million acres of rice land should be developed from formerly uncultivated lands. In order to encourage potential farmers to take the land, given the previous problems with taxes, exemptions from such were granted to the claimers. With this initiative, the larger landholders saw an opportunity for profit and took over great quantities of land, some already, as it turned out, being cultivated by poor farmers. Use of these lands was granted for a period of three generations and then was supposed to revert back to state control, but by 743 it became obvious that these land holdings would be permanently in private hands. Gradually, the individual farmer who worked the smaller tracts saw the necessity for joining with the great landholder in return for protection.

By the end of the ninth century, the large, tax-immune "manors," called *shoen,* had developed to the degree that they had considerable power. *Shomin,* peasants who had joined with the landholders, paid tribute to them, rather than taxes to the government. (Peasants who still held their land privately were called *komin* and were required to pay the comparatively higher state tax, while living under generally worse conditions. They were rapidly fleeing to *shomin* status.) Many landholders eventually had sufficient power to ignore the dictates of the central government in many instances. In turn, the government's ability to keep law and order decreased, making it necessary for the *shoen* to keep men under arms in order to keep the peace in their respective areas. When conditions became more severe, men were trained to perform soldierly duties, and the strength of the resultant "armies" gradually exceeded that of the forces of the government. In fact, these "armies" were called upon by the government in times of rebellion, and their leaders often given posts to keep them on the government's side. It was these warriors who were the forerunners of the samurai class, and the heads of the clans which led them who would become rivals for political power. In any event, the enforcement of law and virtual control of the countryside was steadily passing from the central government to these men trained in the arts of war.

THE CONSOLIDATION OF MILITARY POWER

Two of the clans holding great power in the provinces were the Minamoto (or Genji) and the Taira (or Heike). Both were descended from the imperial family, but their rank had declined through succeeding generations until they had become common soldiers. The Minamoto were originally employed as bodyguards to the Fujiwara, the family which held most of the posts in the central government and which was closest to the emperor, while the Taira were patronized by the retired emperors of the early twelfth century. The men of the two clans were appointed as military leaders, and aspired to high government offices. At the same time, the women sought to marry into the imperial family and be named empress, or at least imperial consort, positions traditionally filled by the Fujiwara. In fact, by 1008, the Minamoto succeeded in having one of their women chosen to be the bride of the new infant emperior, Ichijo.

Minamoto-no-Tsunetomo was the founder of the Minamoto clan. He was a grandson of Emperor Seiwa (r. 858–76) and the son of a prince. Tsunetomo's great-grandson Yoriyoshi was appointed shogun and fought against the Ainu in northern Honshu in the eleventh century. (The title "shogun" did not yet imply that one was military ruler of the entire country, but was used at that time for commanders in campaigns against the Ainu.) Yoriyoshi's son Yoshiie in turn became a warrior and was also appointed shogun. The latter was such a fierce fighter that he was called Hachiman-Taro after the Japanese deity of war. He was successful in conquering the Kanto (Tokyo and surroundings) area.

The Taira family first officially appeared in 889 when Takamochi, a great-grandson of Emperor Kammu (r. 781–806), was given that surname. Taka-mochi settled in the Kanto area and became vice-governor of Kazusa, which lies between present day Tokyo and Chiba. In time, his five sons all settled in that area, and eastern Japan gradually became a stronghold for the Taira. As military men they were proficient so it was only natural that they would become leaders in military affairs.

Until the middle of the twelfth century there was peace and relatively friendly rivalry between the Taira and Minamoto. However, in 1156 the first of the events that were eventually to engage them in a power struggle for control of Japan took place. This was the Hogen Insurrection, which saw elements of the Taira and the Minamoto pitted against the Fujiwara clan. Although the fighting was of short duration, the result was that the Fujiwara were removed as threat to the Taira and Minamoto. Later, from 1159 to 1160, the Heiji War was the first skirmish between the Taira and Minamoto. When the short war was over, the Taira were in a superior position, having installed an emperor who was sympathetic to their cause. As executors of the emperor's will, they held power in the country.

Taira-no-Kiyomori, a high-ranking official in the government, saw the opportunity to increase his own power and influence and that of his family. However, in order to insure his position, he would have to eliminate the only possible threat to his plans, the rival Minamoto. He filled as many of the court offices as he could with his own family members, and was himself appointed chancellor in 1167. Taira power was at its peak in 1168, with high offices in the court held by sixty members of the family. The clan also received tax revenues from some thirty provinces. In 1171 Kiyomori arranged for his daughter to marry Emperor Takakura (r. 1168–80). This maneuver placed him at the summit of his personal power. He had killed his rivals, among them Minamoto-no-Yoshitomo (great-grandson of Yoshiie) and one of Yoshitomo's sons, and scattered the Minamoto clan.

Although Yoshitomo had been killed, Tokiwa, his concubine, had escaped with their three remaining sons. Upon hearing of this, Kiyomori had Tokiwa's mother seized and brought to Kyoto, the capital. He reasoned that Tokiwa's filial piety would prove strong enough so that she would surrender herself rather than see her mother killed. His plan worked; Tokiwa went to Kyoto to save her mother. Kiyomori was so taken with her that he asked her to become his concubine. She refused, but later agreed on the condition that he spare her three sons, a request that Kiyomori finally granted, against the wishes of his retainers. The youngest son, Yoshitsune, escaped Kiyomori's influence and by the age of twenty-one had attained a fine reputation as a soldier. Yoritomo, another of Yoshitomo's sons, was banished by Kiyomori to the province of Izu.

By 1180, Kiyomori's behavior had become unbearable enough that one of the royal princes decided to eliminate him. He sent letters to the heads of the Minamoto clan, hoping that they would support him. Many members of other powerful families, as well as Yoritomo and Yoshitsune, did join him. Thus, the Gempei War (named by combining the "Gen" and "Hei" from "Genji" and "Heike") began.

In one battle, that of Ishibashiyama, Yoritomo was forced to retreat. He gathered other members of his clan and was joined by soldiers of allied clans, eventually raising an army of considerable size and strength. The Taira, hearing of his moves, sent a large army to meet him at Suruga on the Fuji River. Under cover of night the Minamoto attacked and scattered the Taira forces, who subsequently withdrew.

Following this confrontation, Yoritomo set out to develop his seat of power in the area around Kamakura, an old Minamoto home. Within a few months he had built a large city where once had stood only hills and trees. Soon Kamakura became the political as well as the military center of the Kanto Plain. While Yoritomo was thus strengthening his stronghold, his uncle Yukiie, his cousin Yoshinaka, and his brother Yoshitsune headed military expeditions against the enemy. Meanwhile, Taira-no-Kiyomori became ill in Kyoto and died in early 1181. He was succeeded by his son Munemori.

The Minamoto continued their campaign against the Taira, and by mid-1183 a force under Yukiie and Yoshinaka drove the Taira from Kyoto. The Taira fled with the young emperor Antoku and his mother, Kiyomori's daughter. Antoku's brother, Go-Toba, was proclaimed emperor and the wealth of the Taira was divided among the new, Minamoto, rulers.

The military successes and the ensuing ascent to power of Yoshinaka soon went to his head. He refused to obey the mandate of Retired Emperor Go-Shirakawa to hunt down and destroy the remnants of the Taira army. Although he was eventually killed by troops of Yoshitsune, the Taira had regrouped in their stronghold at Fukuhara and had raised a large army in the south and west. The palace at Fukuhara came under seige in 1184 when Yoshitsune led a large force against it. The Taira were driven out, made another stand, in the castle of Yashima, and were forced to flee again. They escaped to the Straits of Shimonoseki and began making preparations for a naval battle.

On the morning of April 25, 1185, the Taira fleet set sail. Although they were experienced in naval warfare, their forces were outnumbered by the Minamoto. Only superior tactics could have brought them victory. Their basic plan was to divide into three groups and use the tide to their advantage. However, in the early afternoon the tide changed, allowing the Minamoto to break through the Taira fleet. The course of the battle turned. Instances of bravery were numerous on both sides. During a lull in the battle, Chikakiyo, a famous Taira archer, fired an arrow into Yoshitsune's ship. When it was retrieved, Yoshitsune asked if any of his archers were capable of firing it back. One, Yoshinari, examined it disdainfully and proclaimed that the arrow was too small. He chose one of his own and fired it back at the Taira boat, killing Chikakiyo. Such fascinating tales are recounted in the *Heike Monogatari*.[1]

As the battle neared its conclusion, the Minamoto, flushed with success, killed most of the Taira. Not content with their victory at sea, they searched the land, killing virtually all the male members of the Taira clan in an effort to wipe out the entire family. Some did escape, to Kyushu, where they lived out their lives, hidden by the rough terrain of the area. Several hundred descendants of the original Taira family were discovered to be living there during the early 1800s.

Yoritomo realized that with a little effort he would be able to consolidate his power and bring most of the country under his control. His creation of the Mandokoro (Council of State) in 1184 allowed him efficient administrative control over the Kanto area. Yoritomo was successful in gaining the support of the officers of the Internal Revenue Department, thereby acquiring a means by which he could finance his new government. He set up criminal courts and rewarded his supporters with government positions. In addition, he asked the emperor to appoint five members of his family to the governorships of provinces. Yoritomo himself was appointed Sei-i Tai Shogun by Emperor Go-Toba in 1192. This title, literally meaning "barbarian-subduing general," now referred to the military ruler of the country.

The rise of the Minamoto and their subsequent assumption of power had placed the military class in a paramount position in Japanese society. The government of the warriors would last until 1867. The final centuries of the rule of the samurai will be taken up in the last section of Chapter 3.

THE SAMURAI CLASS

An examination of the origins of the word "samurai" indicates the original function of those called by that title. The term is derived from the verb *saburou*, which means "to stand by" or "to serve," demonstrating their position of service to an overlord.[2] Understanding how the samurai served will help us to understand the effect that they would ultimately have on modern Japanese society.

Valuable insights into the warrior's life in feudal days can be found in various writings of the times. Among them are *The Documents of Iriki* (1135),[3] the Iriki being a family that settled within the administrative territory of the Satsuma clan. According to the *Documents,* there were several ways of differentiating the samurai as a class from the peasants. In early times the two groups were much alike, with the exception that the samurai could be called to fight for his lord. Since he was under arms, he had the power of law enforcement over commoners in his village. This authority gave him a certain amount of leadership in the area in which he resided. Aside from this, samurai and peasant were similar in their material possessions.

Continuing wars made it possible for some commoners to rise in the ranks to replace the many samurai who were killed off. By the late 1500s it was not unusual to find even the small fief-holder engaged in the military services of his feudal lord. The relatively loose relationship between the samurai and commoners lasted through the sixteenth century. It was accepted, however, that the warriors *(bushi)* were "noble" and the peasants *(domin)* commoners. Up to the fourteenth century all free persons, armed or unarmed, were called *hyakusho,* but after that time the term was applied mainly to the peasantry.

After the sixteenth century the classes became more sharply divided, the peasants being responsible for the working of the land, and the samurai overseeing the control of the land and the collection of revenue. Marriage

Examples of crest designs used by warriors.

between classes was forbidden, and many vassal samurai were shifted to different sections of the country, effectively breaking their relationships with commoners whose families had lived alongside theirs for centuries. This enabled them to rule objectively the lower classes into whose areas they had been moved and served to widen the gap between the classes.

It is interesting to note that in Tokugawa times (1600–1867) a samurai would still be ranked above a rich farmer in theory. Even those samurai who had to till their own small holdings still had more status. What were some of the privileges that went with this superior status? For one thing, the samurai could carry arms. In time the wearing of two swords came to be a symbol of the bearer's class. Another privilege granted to the warrior was the right to a family name. For the most part these names reflected the area from which the family came. A further privilege of the warrior was the use of a family crest, or *mon*. Usually permission for the use of the crest would be granted by the feudal lord. The warrior also frequently bore an official title handed down from prefeudal times. Although most of the titles were supposed to be officially granted, many samurai simply assumed them.

It was the sword which became the badge and symbol of the samurai. The first milestone in a fledgling warrior's life came at the age of five, when he was allowed to wear the costume and wooden fascimile of the real sword of the samurai for the first time. After that he would not be seen in public without his status symbol. After a few years he wore a blunt steel sword daily. By the age of fifteen he was allowed to carry a weapon suitable for any encounter and was considered to be a man. While the constant wearing of a deadly weapon might give rise to abuses of its use, such was not common. The code of the warrior stressed the proper use of the weapon and discouraged its misuse. Because the sword had been used in Japan since early times and since the imperial regalia contained a sword as one of the three sacred treasures, it came to be regarded in military circles as an instrument of justice rather than as a mere weapon.

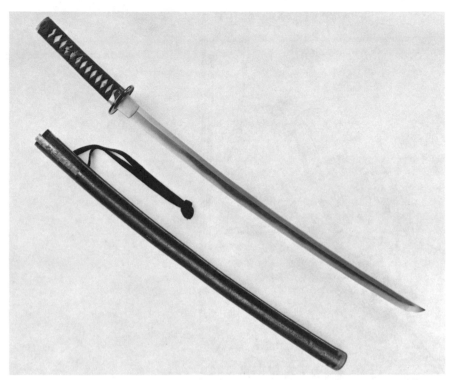

Japanese long sword and scabbard made in 1615 by swordmaker Kunisada Izumo-no-kami. Courtesy of Philadelphia Museum of Art, Edmund L. Zalinsky Collection.

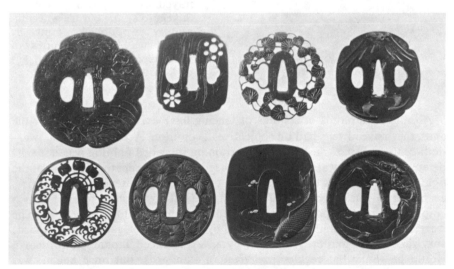

Detail. Examples of handguards, or tsuba, for the long sword. Courtesy of Philadelphia Museum of Art, gift of Mr. C. O. von Kienbusch.

A samurai about to fight portrayed by the actor Nakamura Sukegoro in an eighteenth-century woodblock print by Katsukawa Shunsho. Courtesy of Philadelphia Museum of Art, gift of Mrs. John D. Rockefeller.

Although hundreds of schools of fencing have existed in Japan over the ages, they have always had one objective in common. According to one twentieth-century writer, the objective of training in sword fighting was not self-defense; its primary aim was to allow the fencer to face death.[4] The aim of the fight itself was always the demise of the opponent at whatever cost necessary, even that of one's own life. (This is in contrast to Western fencing, which emphasizes first self-protection, followed by wounding of the opponent.) The warrior's code negated his claim to his own life and relegated it to his lord; survival did not matter. An attack by an experienced Japanese swordsman would be somewhat reckless by Western standards, but once begun, was carried through to its execution in a strong, fierce, decisive move. The Japanese styles of karate—Wado, Shito, Shotokan, and Goju—all evidence the same strong, vigorous attacks whose ultimate goal is the defeat of the opponent. The focus of the training is more philosophical, and like the sword practice, aims at the development of the practitioner's character rather than at superficiality.

BUSHIDO: THE WAY OF THE WARRIOR

The warrior's code alluded to previously evolved in Kamakura (1185–1333) and Muromachi (1338–1573) times; it was an unwritten code of ethics and behavior by which the samurai was supposed to be governed. Its most important point was loyalty to one's lord. This was apparently a direct offshoot of the Confucian tradition of filial piety that had entered Japan from China along with Buddhism in the sixth and seventh centuries. A later writer, Inazo Nitobe, would claim that such a degree of loyalty came from Shinto tradition, however:

> What Buddhism failed to give, Shintoism offered in abundance. Such loyalty to the sovereign, such reverence for ancestral memory, and such filial piety as are not taught by any other creed, were inculcated by the Shinto doctrine, imparting passivity to the otherwise arrogant character of the samurai.[5]

The denial of Chinese influence can be explained by the strong feelings of Japanese nationalism during the period in which Nitobe wrote his book. However, not all historians would agree with Nitobe's view in regard to the motives of the samurai. A completely different view is one which holds that rather than being motivated primarily by loyalty, it is likely that the samurai acted out of personal pride or a desire for fame.[6]

In any case, the loyalty which developed, whether apparent or real, came about at an early time. The benefits to those living on the manors of the large landholders were extensive, including but not limited to security and protection from other feudal lords. Larger estates might have as many as 500 such "retainers," although half that number would be more common. Among their ranks arose two privileged groups, the *ie-no-ko* and the *roto*. The former were blood relations of the lord, and the latter members of the families that had served him for generations.

It should be noted that the loyalty between the lord and his subordinates would have to be reciprocal, or the relationship would be doomed to failure. Such mutual loyalty was evident in many incidents during feudal times. In one such case, the famous Minamoto-no-Yoshiie (1041–1108) left an important clan meeting to avenge an insult to one of his *roto*. He returned to his manor from a neighboring province and burned the offender's mansion the day after the insult was committed. Such immediate action demonstrated the extent to which the tradition had developed at that early time. Loyalty to one's *roto* was instrumental in building the power base that had enabled the Minamoto to ascend to the leadership of the country.

It was not until Tokugawa times, however, that the code of ethics encompassing such loyalty became known as bushido, the "way of the warrior." This was the result of the attempt on Shogun Tokugawa Ieyasu's part to set down regulations for the samurai class in his *Laws for the Military Houses*. In succeeding years additional virtues were added by other shogun until a firm code of ethics evolved.

Although the concept of bushido is not difficult to define in general terms (e.g., as a "code of ethics"), it may be observed that the view of it differs according to the intent of authors who set out to treat the subject. There are those who glorify Japanese culture, describing bushido in terms of a set of behavioral norms that seem consistent with the highest ideals of mankind in general. Nitobe wrote: "In manifold ways had Bushido filtered down from the social class where it orginated . . . furnishing a moral standard for the whole people."[7] He saw bushido as a powerful social force that had shaped Japan and helped her survive in the face of adversity.

Opposed to this school of thought are those who saw bushido as nothing more than rationalization for murder and crimes against the populace, the perverted norms of a group of ruthless overlords intent on brutalizing the lower classes. Such a view was espoused by E. H. Norman, who described samurai as men who viewed the commoner as a subhuman being who could be killed for any slight, either real or imagined. The lower classes existed only at the pleasure of the samurai and could be disposed of at will.[8]

Although a case may be made for either extreme, it is not the purpose here to explore the controversies over the nature of the samurai class and its code of bushido, but rather to investigate the concept of bushido itself. Further, if the elements of the code of bushido remained unchanged over a long period of time, then it will be relatively easy to determine just what the traditional Japanese conception of the code has been.

The first of the useful source materials, presented here in chronological order, is "The Imagawa Letter."[9] It consists of a series of admonitions by Imagawa Sadayo to his adopted son Naka-aki. The letter, dating from approximately 1412, advised the young man that the arts of war alone were not sufficient to govern correctly. In order to do so, it was necessary to study the arts of peace. In particular, he referred to the study of Chinese political philosophy, law, Japanese and Chinese history, and Zen philosophy. These would prepare the samurai for a position of leadership. Thus, at that early time some samurai valued literacy, especially for the higher-ranked members of the class. Other ideals encouraged in the latter articles of the Letter included duty, fairness, filial piety, justice, loyalty, discretion, correct moral behavior, frugality, courage, skill in the martial arts, and what Imagawa described as the essential virtues of human-heartedness, righteousness, propriety, wisdom, and good faith.

From a late-sixteenth-century samurai leader we have a list of seven ordinances.[10] Kato Kiyomasa, one of Toyotomi Hideyoshi's top generals, advised soldiers to be skilled in martial arts, to rise early and practice with sword, spear, and bow-and-arrow till noon; after lunch the musket and equestrian skills were to be practiced. Pastimes for the samurai should be limited to hawking, deer hunting, wrestling, and similar sports. The life of a samurai should display frugality in all things; he should dress in cotton or pongee, not have parties, and not engage in unseemly behavior. Literary endeavors should be limited to reading books on military subjects, loyalty, and filial piety. The writing of poetry was considered effeminate.

Perhaps the most well-known source on the traditions of the samurai class is the "Buke Shohatto" of 1615.[11] Included among the rules listed are the ideas that *bun* and *bu* (literary and military skills) should be combined; that drunkenness, gambling, and other loose behavior was forbidden; that clothing should be plain and appropriate to the wearer's rank; and in general that the warrior should live a simple life. In addition, the samurai's behavior should exemplify the cardinal virtues of loyalty and obedience.

A later writer, Yamaga Soko (1622–85), was a powerful influence on the traditions of the military men. In his work *Shido,* Yamaga saw the primary mission of the samurai as service, making it essential that he understood his role. The classes beneath him saw in the samurai a virtuous role model to be emulated, and in his way an exemplary pattern of behavior that they could follow.[12] The work of Yamaga represented a transition in the role of the samurai. No longer was it sufficient for the warrior to study martial arts and traditional subjects. He must also learn how to govern, which meant an increasing amount of education in bureaucratic matters. Additionally, the modes of behavior that guided the samurai class were no longer to be the exclusive property of that group.

This example-setting role was repeated throughout the Tokugawa period by other philosophers and teachers, one of whom was Hosoi Heishu (1728–1801). Hosoi was one of many whose job was to inculcate in the minds of the lower classes the virtues of the samurai. He had been educated in the Confucian classics as a young man and was well known as one of the most popular of the contemporary neo-Confucian teachers. His work was officially sanctioned by the domain governments, who realized that the samurai's values of loyalty to his lord, filial piety, frugality, and self-discipline, coupled with an overriding sense of duty, would assist in maintaining stability in the country. One of his sermons, given in 1783, placed particular emphasis on the values of obedience and filial piety.[13]

Shortly after the Meiji Restoration (1868), at which time the government of the samurai was dissolved, these ideals, traditionally held as the guiding light of the samurai, were once again presented to the lower classes as their inheritance from the warrior. Amane Nishi (1829–97) wrote the "Gunjin Kunkai" (Admonition to Soldiers) at the request of General Aritomo Yamagata (1838–1922), a member of a samurai family.[14] This document advised soldiers to practice loyalty, obedience, and bravery and stressed that the modern soldier was the same as the samurai of former times. Thus, the tradition of the samurai class was given to the modern conscript army as its own.

In 1882 the "Imperial Rescript to Soldiers and Sailors" was issued. Behind this document also was the thought of General Yamagata. It simply codified the values of bushido that Yamagata had learned during his youth and applied them to the construction of a modern military ethos. Within the Imperial Rescript is found conclusive evidence that the values of the past were to be ultilized in the new Japan. The first article held that loyalty was the essential duty of the soldier and sailor, reflecting the long tradition of vassal-lord relations that existed in Japan since earlier times.[15] Since the hallmark of the fighting man was courage, it was to be expected that this element would be found in the Imperial Rescript also. Article three stated that the modern warrior was encouraged to view valor as a trait to be admired. Reckless behavior in the face of the enemy was not desirable; however, the soldier

The archer Wada Raihachi portrayed by the actor Ichikawa Ebijuro I in an early nineteenth-century woodblock print by Hokushu. Courtesy of the Philadelphia Museum of Art; print purchased by subscription, supplemented by the Lola Downin Peck Fund.

should be able to act discriminately and correctly in battle. The article further advised that the performance of duty was one of the more valorous acts. The fourth article told conscripts that faithfulness in the keeping of one's word and righteousness in fulfilling one's duty were to be honored. Still another traditional samurai value, simplicity, was emphasized in the fifth article. Luxury and extravagance were considered effeminate and would not add to the correct performance of duty. Rather, they would turn the soldier into one who sought material things at the expense of his duty. In addition to these basic admonitions, there was concern over sincerity. A sincere effort on the part of the conscript would allow great achievement.

Hardly two decades had passed when those values were reiterated by Inazo Nitobe. In his book *Bushido: The Soul of Japan,* published at the turn of the century, Nitobe stressed that the values of the samurai centered on wisdom, benevolence, courage, frugality, and moral righteousness. As with earlier writers, he felt that the samurai had set examples for others to follow. "The precepts of Knighthood, begun at first as the glory of the elite, became in time an aspiration and inspiration to the nation at large."[16]

The discussion so far has involved a general survey of original thinkers and more modern writers in an attempt to discover if there are any definite characteristics of bushido that persisted during the Tokugawa and Meiji (1868–1912) periods. Note, though, that the concept of bushido was an idealized pattern of behavior that all members of society could revere as a set of guiding principles as they struggled to find order in a culture that did not provide an easy existence for them. In the case of the samurai, as they grew out of their original role as warriors and into more modern times, the ideal came to be viewed with an almost religious fervor. It grew in magnitude to the point that perfection would have been necessary in order to follow its precepts. The existence of this problem is evident in the many edicts and documents produced to teach people this ideal behavior. (The "Buke Shohatto," mentioned previously, was only one of many such documents.)

The set of norms which bushido comprises seems to have remained consistent throughout a period of several centuries, even though some details may have been altered. Although specific situations may have called for the inclusion or exclusion of some of the following, they nonetheless represent a basic listing of the component parts of the code of bushido. They include frugality, stoicism, honor, benevolence, obedience, a sense of duty, a warlike spirit, loyalty, courage, a sense of morality, self-discipline, decorum, sobriety, honesty, practical ethics, and the study of war and administration. Many of these aspects are evident in Japanese society today.

THE ZEN TRADITION

Those who find the military exploits of the samurai of interest are frequently exposed in print to the subject of the "religion" of the samurai. Although it has been claimed that bushido was a religion,[17] it is better termed a code of ethics. If it can be said that the samurai had any religion at all, then it is Zen Buddhism which must be examined.

The first of the Zen sects to be introduced to Japan was the Rinzai sect. It was brought in 1191 by Eisai (1141–1215), a Japanese monk who was dissatisfied with the doctrines of his school and who had thus journeyed to China to study. Upon his return, he founded two monasteries that would be devoted to the study of the new "meditation school." The Rinzai sect has traditionally used the *koan,* a sort of riddle, to assist meditating students in the achievement of *satori,* or enlightenment. A *koan* could only be answered satisfactorily if the answer were spontaneous and showed understanding of Zen principles. Students would perform *zazen,* that is, meditation in a seated position. During such a session, a student would have to concentrate on a *koan* or keep his mind clear by focusing on a single word or sound. Such methods might lead to an instantaneous *satori.*

The second major Zen sect, the Soto, was founded by Dogen (1200–53). He was also a monk who had journeyed to China to increase his knowledge of Buddhism. His return to Japan in 1228 left him disillusioned, so he sought seclusion in the northern districts, where in addition to teaching student monks, he gave instruction to samurai as well. Soto differed from Rinzai in that it claimed that the attainment of enlightenment was a gradual process, rather than a sudden one as in Rinzai *satori.*

The introduction of Zen coincided roughly with the ascent of the warrior class to supremacy in Japanese society. It was necessary for these new warrior-administrators to have a religion that would serve their needs, one that would give them the mental and spiritual discipline necessary to fulfill their new functions in society. That the original Buddhist sects, with their emphasis on piety and the study of scriptures, had not appealed to the samurai is easily understood. Only Zen offered a means by which a man might control his own destiny. On the practical level, it taught the soldier to concentrate single-mindedly on the attack and not to think of defeat. It also stressed self-discipline and inner control, strengthened by meditation, in order that the samurai might achieve enlightenment.

Although Zen played a significant role in the life of the samurai, the exact nature of the role was somewhat unique. The focus of a samurai's Zen training was to attain the state of *mushin,* "no-mind," in which the human concerns of everyday life, even the concerns over life itself, were viewed as insignificant. However, even though he followed a mystical path to salvation, he was, of course, affected by social forces. What Zen did was to prepare him for his position in society. In more modern thought, the samurai would fit Max Weber's description of an "inner world mystic";[18] there would be no attempt on his part to escape involvement in the world's affairs, but he would place no significance on events that affected his daily life. He had to look within himself for the rationalization of his life's actions, rather than to a noble cause for which he could devote himself.

This concept of no-mind was particularly important to the samurai attempting to perfect sword-fighting techniques. If he concentrated on his own or his opponent's actions in order to fight effectively, his movements would not be spontaneous. Fear of dying or defeat could also cloud his mind. He practiced Zen in order to control these natural urges. Training in Zen eliminated the division between the swordsman and his sword by elimination of the consciousness that identified each. Thus they became one, allowing the highest skill in technique.

In his letter to Yagyu Munenori (1571–1646), one of Japan's greatest swordsmen, the famous Zen monk Takuan (1573–1645) described the process by which fencers reached perfection of their art.[19] According to him, beginners and experts shared the same type of mind. Since the beginner knew no techniques, he did not think, but simply responded to an attack. In like manner the expert swordsman who had mastered his technique would also respond instantly. It was the swordsman beyond the beginner stage who had not mastered *mushin* that had the problem. He knew enough to recognize the possibilities and therefore his mind was clouded by thought. The spontaneity of the expert swordsman had to be the same as the spontaneity required to answer a *koan*. Ideally, his technique would be a combination of Zen and practical training with the sword.

Miyamoto Musashi (1584–1645) also expounded the idea of *mushin*. Known as Kensei, or "sword saint," he had studied Zen during his youth under a local priest. He later won over sixty duels and killed many more men in actual combat. Toward the end of his life he wrote *A Book of Five Rings,* or *Go Rin no Sho,* in which he discussed the correct state of mind a warrior needed when facing an opponent.[20] Such a mind was one that is unclouded by thought, a "void" in which the mind has been cleared of all confusion.

As a final note on sources describing the relationship between Zen and the martial arts, Eugen Herrigel's *Zen in the Art of Archery* is mentioned.[21] In this work the author, a German philosopher who traveled to Japan to teach and who began the practice of archery to further his understanding of Zen, details how the philosophy and the art are connected. By comparison, it is interesting to note that no literature describing medieval European warriors ever mentions a connection between martial arts and philosophy in any way similar to that of the Japanese.

So far, we have discussed the ideal aspired to by the individual fighting man of Japan. Just how widespread was the actual mastery of Zen by samurai in Japan's feudal period? There was no guarantee that the average samurai achieved the ultimate enlightenment that Zen offered, as it would require great effort in the study of the precepts of Buddhism alone. Indeed, it is probable that mastery of the concept of *mushin* was the possession of only the top sword, spear, and bow masters who managed to combine within their training the same methods used to achieve enlightenment by the monks in their mountain retreats. There are few names in the annals of Japanese history that stand out as invincible wielders of the sword or other weapons, giving rise to the speculation that perhaps only a small percentage of those belonging to the class were able to couple fully their mastery of weapons with Zen. The major effect of Zen then was to set an ideal to be sought after, that is, a goal not attainable by all, but nonetheless held in great esteem by all as the ultimate focus of their training. We may also see in such an aspiration a rationalization for the deeds performed by the warrior in his service to his lord. The individual's self-abnegation was seen as the true core of the samurai's being, an attribute highly valued and sought after because not all could attain it.

3

Samurai Customs and Traditions

SEPPUKU

The most spectacular and perhaps best-known tradition of the Japanese samurai was the ritual suicide known as seppuku. Historical accounts of Japanese warriors abound with grisly descriptions of how it was performed, and the reader can only wonder at the culture that spawned such a practice. Seppuku was the samurai's way of saving face, atoning for his trespasses, or even at times a method of proving his sincerity. Known in the West by the vulgarism hara-kiri (lit., belly-cutting), it involved the cutting of the abdomen.

If a samurai were truly loyal to his lord, he would be willing to perform the act without question. In most cases, of course, there was a reason. The condemned man might have committed some trespass or may have failed in his duty. Even if caught in some criminal activity, the taking of his own life was his birthright. Faced with capture on the field of battle, the samurai would kill himself rather than be taken prisoner, thereby denying the satisfaction of victory to his enemy. His method of suicide was an open display of courage and also an act of defiance. On occasion, the samurai might cause his own destruction in order to emphasize a point with his lord or make known the strength of his convictions. While abandoning one's life in such a manner might seem drastic to Western readers, the samurai did not have the same difficulty that a non-samurai might have. His life was not his own and, therefore, he had not a life to surrender. If the act in some way assisted his lord in a campaign or decision, then he had served admirably well and had fulfilled his role in society.

The ceremony of seppuku was a formal one. Numerous accounts of the procedure exist and relate in great detail how it was performed. At the appointed time, the condemned man was led to a courtyard in front of many witnesses. Kneeling in the center with a stick between his thighs and calves to insure that he would collapse forward, he turned his jacket back down over his shoulders, baring himself to the waist. In front of him was his short sword wrapped in clean rice paper and placed on a stand near the ground. Taking the short sword in his right hand, he plunged it into the left side of his abdomen and cut horizontally across his stomach. If he did not pass out at that point, he then withdrew the blade and made a vertical cut in the same manner, in order to carve a cross mark. At that point, he would be close to passing out from pain and loss of blood. This was a crucial time. His second, called a *kaishakunin,* stood behind him, sword in hand, ready to finish the act by cutting off the seppuku performer's head. If he did not perform the decapitation successfully, or if the body hit the ground before he performed the cut, the *kaishakunin* was disgraced.

The custom underwent many changes throughout Japanese history. In certain times, only one cut would be performed before the decapitation, while in others the decapitation would be done as soon as the dagger had broken the skin. The would-be suicide was spared the agony of his own doing in some ages, when a fan replaced the short sword and he did not have to cut himself at all. The latter method came into vogue during the Tokugawa period as Japan became more settled and the wars that had given the samurai his bloody heritage abated.[1]

Up to and through the early years of the Tokugawa shogunate, it was not uncommon for samurai to kill themselves when their lord died. Called *oibara,* this was considered an honorable act that fulfilled the duty of the samurai to his lord. In 1663 the shogunate prohibited the practice in order to save the needless loss of life. Five years later, in violation of the prohibition, a samurai named Sugiura committed the act. The shogunate decided to make an example of him and thus executed four members of his family and banished the rest, effectively discouraging the practice of *oibara* from that time forward. There was, however, a singular revival in 1912 when General Nogi and his wife committed suicide upon the death of Emperor Meiji.

The wife of a samurai was often a partner in the act. Upon the death of her husband, she would usually take her life, but not by so gruesome a method. In most cases she tied her ankles together with a long sash or cord to keep from being found in an unseemly position in death. She then knelt down and cut her jugular vein with a short knife, thereby following her husband on the final journey.

VENDETTAS

The carrying out of a vendetta among samurai was a common practice. In part it was influenced by pride, a desire for revenge on a personal basis, loyalty to one's lord, or in the case of a parent, filial piety and the Confucian ethic. Matters that had to be settled between samurai usually called for a duel, although in some instances a samurai might hunt down his man and kill him in a surprise attack. The victim's nearest kin would then be duty-bound to find the assailant and seek revenge. There was no law proscribing this, and in cases when the offender was a paid retainer, the avenging samurai would request permission for a public duel. This would rule out any controversy, legal or otherwise, over the act. Supposedly, the lord of the retainer would insure that fair play was observed. Women were also known to seek revenge on slayers of members of their family. In fact, the act of revenge was considered such a duty that it almost had the standing of law. The most famous vendetta was the deed of the 47 Ronin, carried out by loyal retainers in the best tradition of the class. Their story will be recounted briefly here.

It was an established custom of the Tokugawa shogunate to receive tribute from its feudal lords once a year, enabling the shogunate to maintain control over the land. In like manner, the shogun paid tribute to the imperial court at Kyoto. The gifts consisted of sums of money and other items. In return, the emperor would send envoys to the shogun's castle to return the courtesy. These envoys had to be entertained and served, a job which was given to appointed members of the upper ruling class, the daimyo. From among the daimyo, two were chosen to serve in this host capacity each year. Although the position involved a great expense and was difficult, it was considered a great honor and was highly prized for the prestige that it brought.

In 1701, Asano Takumi-no-kami, Lord of Ako, was appointed to the position. Although he was honored to receive the appointment, he asked to be relieved, since he was a country samurai and not well versed in the manners and customs of court life (and was not at all wealthy). Asano was told that his case was not unusual, however, since most samurai were not familiar with the court procedures, and so Shogun Tsunayoshi assigned the Grand Master of Ceremonies to him, to ensure that he was taught the correct procedures. The Grand Master of Ceremonies was Kira Kozuke-no-suke, of *hatamoto* rank, one step below daimyo. Kira used the position to obtain bribes from the lords that he served. Although this was not supposed to be done, everyone understood the expenses of his position and nothing was done to prevent the practice.

Kira's other charge, Daté, Lord of Yoshida, was a young man who was well advised by his elder retainers. They understood Kira's position and prepared substantial bribes in order to have the Grand Master do his best for their lord. This led Kira to expect the same type of reward from Asano. Unfortunately, the bribe did not materialize: he was presented with a token present, which insulted him. To take revenge, Kira deliberately misinformed Asano and caused him to commit several serious breaches of etiquette. When Asano sought advice from others in the court, Kira insulted him publicly on several occasions. Asano could no longer bear this, so even though he was in the midst of the ceremonies with the emperor's envoys, he drew his sword and struck Kira, wounding him.

The shogun was so enraged—since drawing a sword (and even quarreling) in the castle compound was illegal—that he ordered Asano to commit seppuku at once, barely giving him time to write a farewell to his head retainer, Kataoka Gengoemon. Such a sentence might have been acceptable to the young lord, but his antagonist, Kira, was praised for his behavior and allowed to go unpunished. In addition, the Asano family name was made extinct and their holdings confiscated. This meant that the samurai who had served the Lord of Ako were now without a master. They had in the space of a few days become *ronin,* masterless samurai. Oishi Kura-no-suke, the chief councillor in charge of the Asano castle, swore revenge. At a meeting of some three hundred of the new *ronin,* it was decided that Kira should not be allowed to live. In such a case it was expected that the former retainers of Ako would seek revenge, and the home of Kira was sure to be closely guarded. Therefore, the conspirators decided to wait.

Since there were over three hundred men in the Asano group, it was at first thought that while they were waiting, they might be able to hold on to their lord's castle if the shogun's men tried to seize it. However, it came out in subsequent meetings that many of the samurai were not willing to take this course of action. In a short time their number had dwindled to sixty-one. Realizing that they could do little to stop a take-over with so few men, they signed an oath to take revenge on Kira. Of that number, only forty-seven would eventually be involved in the plot to assassinate him. They disbanded and met two years later in Edo to carry out their plan. Under cover of night they attacked Kira's mansion and succeeded in killing him. His head was cut off and mounted on a spear. It was then carried to the Asano family tomb at Takanawa and placed on the grave of their lord. Each of the forty-seven struck the head three times with their daggers and the ceremony was completed. They then reported their act of vengeance to the Inspector General, Lord Sengoku, who took them into custody.

Their act and subsequent surrender caused a great deal of trouble for the shogun. They had violated the law and were guilty of murder; however, they had lived up to the best traditions of the samurai class and had not allowed their lord's death to go unavenged. They were living examples of the saying "no man should live under the same sky with the slayer of his father or lord." There was great sympathy on the part of the authorities and the public for them. After a year's debate, it was decided that they should die for violating the law, but not as common criminals. Since they were samurai, they would be allowed to commit seppuku.

On February 4, 1703, all forty-seven of the *ronin* knelt in the courtyards of the lords in whose custody they had been placed and ended their lives in the most traditional fashion. Thus they passed into history as eminent examples of the Japanese fighting man.

THE CHANGING OF TRADITION

Prior to the advent of the Tokugawa rule in 1600, Japan experienced a series of internecine battles that eventually led to the grand campaign for the unification of the nation. In those times a samurai was continually ready for war—if not a major campaign, then perhaps one against the neighboring estate in a quest for land desired by his lord. This incessant warfare meant that the cult of the warrior was continually strengthened and reinforced. Samurai were expected to live frugal lives in the most stoic fashion. The use of colorful clothing was proscribed, as were singing, poetry, and other so-called vices, all of which were considered effeminite. It was thought that these endeavors would soften the soldier and make him psychologically and physically unfit to serve. Thus, the arts of war and physical exercise were encouraged, and a somber and difficult life prevailed for the warrior.

Once the country had been unified by the Tokugawa and there was relative peace, however, the need for the services of the samurai as a warrior diminished. Administration of the fief and fulfillment of many government and domain positions required men who were not only born to rank, but who were also capable of performing the tasks required. In order to prepare for these positions, samurai became literate, so much so in fact, that literacy came to be considered as important as martial arts. The saying "pen and sword in accord" reflected the new emphasis on this balance. Thus, the philosophy of *bun* and *bu* (literary and military), together, came about.

Of course, it had always been necessary to have literate members of the class administer the feudal estate; however, this was a relatively simple matter when compared to the complex system of administration that existed in Tokugawa times. This involved strict accounting of finances by all feudal lords so that they would not be able to amass enough money to threaten Tokugawa rule. To further control them, the feudal lords were classed into three groups: *shimpan,* or related lords; *fudai daimyo,* hereditary vassals; and *tozama,* outside lords. The *shimpan* were members of the Tokugawa clan and were therefore highly trusted. The *fudai daimyo* were lords who had previously been allied with the Tokugawa and were thus also trusted by them. After the consolidation of power, they were given fiefs around the Tokugawa stronghold at Edo so as to insulate it from attack. Other members of the *fudai daimyo* were given strategic land holdings to keep enemies under surveillance. The *tozama* were those lords who had either fought against the Tokugawa or who had joined them after the battle of Sekigahara, the decisive battle in 1600 which had brought the Tokugawa to power. They were under suspicion, so their land was redistributed in order that they could be kept under constant surveillance. The complexities involved in the administration of such a system necessarily gave rise to certain changes in the nature of the samurai class, among them a rise in the literacy rate.

An additional obstacle to be overcome was the traditional association of literacy with business transactions and the merchant class. In traditional Confucian-oriented Japanese society, the merchant class was at the bottom of the social ladder, beneath artisans, peasants, and samurai. This was because the merchant produced nothing; he only bought, sold, and traded goods produced by others. For a samurai to adopt the skills of the class at the opposite end of the social scale would be difficult.

At the beginning of the Tokugawa era, the education that existed in Japan centered largely around the *terakoya,* or temple school. Since samurai were not engaged in literary endeavors in earlier times, it was the Buddhist temples and monasteries that had become the centers of intellectual pursuit. These temple schools gradually increased in number and were supplemented by the establishment of *han,* or fief, schools. These were deemed valuable, since they provided the means to train future administrators from among the samurai and also would be useful in keeping the samurai under control. Toward the nineteenth century, the samurai class became even more literate through the founding of additional *han* schools.

An earlier tradition of education also persisted into the Tokugawa period. This was the means by which bushido was able to be passed on. During the first few years of a young samurai's life, his father would assign a woman to care for him, a type of live-in nurse known as a *menoto*. The *menoto* was charged with basic care of the child and was usually the daughter of a samurai who served the estate. Many of the *menoto* had children of their own that they cared for along with the samurai's child, thereby creating a close bond between their children and those of the lord. That relationship strengthened the feudal system and made it more familial. Since the *menoto* had great influence on these children, they were held in high esteem and were actually responsible for passing on to the youths the traditions of the class. The role of women as carriers of tradition seems to have persisted until the turn of the present century at least. In an unpublished article in the Griffis Collection, a scene is described in which a Japanese mother gives advice to her son on the eve of his departure for the Russo-Japanese War.[2] She reminded him of the traditions of his ancestors and indicated that certain things would be expected of him. What was desired of course, was that he would live up to the bushido code of the feudal samurai class. In this manner the value system of the Tokugawa samurai was carried forward to twentieth-century Japan.

THE SAMURAI IN TRANSITION

Congruent with tradition in pre-modern Japan, one automatically became a samurai if one was born into a samurai family. Furthermore, the Japanese warrior claimed the privilege of class as a birthright; that is, merchants, peasants, and artisans could not join this exclusive group. There were, however, deviations from this norm that shall be considered below. It may be asked whether men of ability were able to rise in the ranks to become samurai, even if they had been born as peasants or merchants. As one might suspect, movement between social strata would be more difficult in a stable society than in one beset by internal wars and revolutions.

In the late twelfth century, Shogun Minamoto-no-Yoritomo had issued a set of regulations identifying the samurai and his role in society and proscribing entrance into the class without the express permission of the shogun. Even so, four more centuries of intermittent warfare made it possible to rise in status from the lower classes to that of warrior. However, this was to end with the unification of Japan under the Tokugawa and the settling of the nation's internal problems. The Tokugawa shogunate saw the easy entrance of lower classes into the samurai ranks that had been possible in times of war as an unsettling factor in Japanese society. Therefore, it sought to bring the situation under control. It pressured the existing samurai to leave the land and accept positions living in the castle towns, where they would receive stipends and be under the control of the local daimyo. It also set up strict regulations that prohibited entrance into the class. Representatives of the shogunate were energetic in their enforcement of the regulation and the opportunities for rising on the social scale were severely limited.

Thus, Japanese society became stabilized, and the class structure followed more closely a Confucian model. The warrior administrators were still the power class in society and the peasants, artisans, and the merchants followed in the order. (Although the merchant class was considered the lowest, the financial dealings of that group were to give them a great deal of power, which would increase as the Tokugawa period wore on.) With entrance into the samurai ranks officially closed, there were few avenues left to the commoner who sought to raise his status. In some cases men of exceptional ability might be adopted by a samurai family in need of money or an heir; however, for the most part adoption was used to raise ones position from that of low-ranked samurai to a higher rank within the class.[3]

What were the differences in official rank within the samurai class, and to what degree did mobility exist between these ranks? There is, in fact, little agreement among writers over the centuries on the types of rank and their definition, since most samurai were not employed by the emperor or the shogun, but were in fact retainers of one of the approximately 265 daimyo who ruled the various *han* throughout Japan. (The number of daimyo changed during the various shogunates.) Widely different rankings existed, according to the size and wealth of the *han*.

Before outlining the official ranks, it should be noted that such rank was not the main determinant of social status within the class; instead, the income of the samurai family (their rice stipend, measured in *koku*—a unit of about five bushels) was the chief indicator. It will be noted below that yearly income did not always depend on official rank. Further complications came into play as well. For example, under the Japanese system of unitary inheritance, the majority of one's estate was passed along to only one son—the best qualified, not necessarily the eldest.[4] A family with an annual stipend of 100 *koku,* but with no son, might adopt one of the sons from a family with an income of 200 *koku.* If the boy had stayed with his own family, he might have received almost nothing as an inheritance. Therefore, adoption into a family that would provide him with the opportunity to become its head would be considered upward social mobility, even though the family he was joining was lower in status than his own when measured in terms of income.

Most scholars would agree that the samurai class might be divided into upper, middle, and lower classes, but the boundaries of these groupings are often disputed, especially in the case of the latter two. The upper-class samurai consisted of the daimyo and the branch families of the Tokugawa clan. As the ruling elite of the capital and the province, these samurai would have the largest incomes and the most power. In fact, they may be called the upper-upper class. Directly under them were the senior vassals who held the top administrative posts under the Tokugawa and who had significantly high incomes. To determine the extent of the incomes of those upper samurai is difficult; the range might be from a few hundred to over ten thousand *koku,* depending on the size and wealth of the domain.

Beneath the upper samurai in rank were what might be termed the middle samurai, consisting mainly of *hatamoto* (bannermen) and *hirazamurai* (ordinary samurai). (There are some writers who would call the *hatamoto* lower-upper class.) They held fiefs whose annual yield was rarely more than 3,000 *koku* and sometimes down to a few hundred, and had direct rights of audience with their lord. Their personal income might range from as little as twenty *koku* and up to three hundred. Beneath them were the lower samurai, consisting of *ashigaru* (foot soldiers), *baishin* (rear vassals), and *goshi* (rural samurai). The *ashigaru* were the upper-lower class and held positions in the civil service equivalent to messengers and clerks, in addition to their regular military duties. Their income might be from three to twelve *koku* per annum. The *baishin* were retainers of senior families who still held land in the fief. Their income was from four to one hundred fifty *koku.* The last group, the *goshi,* were the remnants of the original farmer-warrior class that had largely

A young samurai on horseback depicted in an eighteenth-century woodblock print by Suzuki Harunobu. Courtesy of Philadelphia Museum of Art, gift of Mrs. John D. Rockefeller.

been replaced over the centuries. They resided in the countryside and had stipends of no more than five *koku*.

Under these conditions, social mobility was severely limited. Men of great ability might, under certain circumstances, achieve a rise in status, but in large part the ranks were frozen. Some mobility in a downward direction might have occurred, however, if a samurai failed to carry out the functions of his role due to ill health or other unfortunate circumstances. In some cases downward mobility was instituted as a form of punishment. Individuals might, on the basis of their own ability, move within the rank structure, but the major part of such movement was within each of the three major divisions.

As previously mentioned, movement into the samurai class became very difficult in the early Tokugawa years. However, when entrance of commoners into the warrior elite began to occur with increasing regularity toward the end of the Tokugawa period, it was cause for great alarm. The ability of commoners to ascend the social ladder may be seen as a direct result of the early Tokugawa efforts to remove the samurai from the land and make them paid retainers, rather than farmer-warriors as they had been in times past. This was done to prevent downward mobility of the lower samurai and the possible formation of a new gentry class of ex-samurai. Therefore, *hatamoto* whose income was less than 500 *koku* of rice were usually withdrawn from the land and given a fixed stipend by the local daimyo. This was acceptable to many, and by 1722 it is estimated that fewer than one-tenth of the *hatamoto* were still on the land and not in the castle towns with the rest of their class. With their new free time, many samurai became more literate in an attempt to equalify for higher positions in the central and *han* bureaucracies.

As towns and cities grew in size, the merchant class increased its wealth and influence. Many daimyo found themselves indebted to the newly wealthy merchants and attempted to pay off their debts by borrowing money from their retainers. The "loans," whose principal was obtained by withholding up to sixty percent of the rice stipend paid to the retainer, were involuntary and were never paid back. Since the effect of these permanent loans was to reduce the already meager incomes of many of the samurai, they, in turn, became indebted and disenchanted with their status in society and with their lords. Faced with such difficulties, samurai would sometimes eradicate their financial distress by adopting the son of a wealthy merchant in exchange for a substantial sum from the aspiring samurai's father. By the end of Tokugawa times this practice had become fairly common and was no longer officially decried by the shogunate. The situation had worsened so much that by 1850 the adoption fees for entry of commoners into the samurai ranks were widely known. Ascent into the samurai class was now possible for even the lowest and most disreputable members of the society as long as they were capable of producing the requisite entrance fees.

Lest it be assumed that mobility involved only commoners, it should be mentioned that it was not unusual at that time for a samurai to relinquish his status to become a member of the merchant class. In most cases, this provided to be financially advantageous. As far as class and rank were concerned, the mobility would be downward; however, if income were considered, the reverse would be true. Surveying the transition of the samurai from fighting man par excellence to peacetime warrior to government administrator may leave the impression of viewing the decline and fall of a class. Actually, the opposite is true. Rather than declining in power and influence, the samurai adapted themselves to the changing conditions of Japanese society as it began to modernize and ultimately provided the Japan that emerged in the twentieth century with bureaucratic and intellectual leadership.

The final phase of the samurai change can be seen as a transition of class structures, or a sort of mass social mobility. After the Meiji Restoration of 1868, the samurai and other classes in society were reclassified as *shizoku* (gentry) and *heimin* (commoners), respectively. Further declassification came in 1871, after which it was decreed that samurai could voluntarily give up wearing their swords. This was part of the government's samurai rehabilitation program, which aimed at absorbing former samurai into society at large. As a part of program, the Meiji government passed a law that allowed samurai to enter into any occupation they desired; the downward social mobility of the once priviliged class was now officially approved by the new government. The ability of the lower classes to advance in government was also legitimatized during the years following the Meiji Restoration. The philosophy of the new government was based on the idea that all men in society were equal and could be useful to the state if their ability was sufficient. This paved the way for a new conscript army, which put an official end to the elite military class that had ruled Japan for the better part of seven centuries. According to the government declaration on military conscription in 1872, the age-old delineation of class no longer existed.

Holdouts among the samurai, however, refused to go along with the new political process, and a last attempt was made to overthrow the Meiji government by Takamori Saigo. A samurai of the Satsuma clan, Takamori led a band of some fifteen thousand samurai troops into Kagoshima in January 1877. After successfully capturing government depots there, they turned northward to Kumamoto where they met strong resistance from the imperial forces holding Kumamoto Castle. As the situation seemed serious, the Imperial government committed its entire army of thirty-two thousand men against the rebels and was able to defeat them. Although the government had expended over forty-two million yen and had taken nine months to stop the insurrection, the victory was of great significance. The modern conscript army had faced seasoned samurai warriors and had emerged victorious. Claims of samurai invincibility would be hard to prove from that time on.

4

Karate and Japanese Martial Arts Traditions

When karate was introduced to Japan in 1922, it began a long and subtle change, a change that was to be marked by the adoption of certain Japanese cultural traits, among them the basic traditions of the samurai. Since by this time the traditions of the samurai class had filtered down to the level of the common man and had been adopted by the Japanese nation as a whole, karate-do, in becoming a part of Japanese culture, was influenced by this samurai ethos, including the Confucian traditions of filial piety, the "way of the warrior" itself, and Zen.

JAPANESE ADAPTATIONS OF CHINESE PHILOSOPHY

The Confucian influence upon karate is obvious in any dojo where there is a native Japanese teacher. The head instructor is seen as a father figure, all wise and knowing and the model of fairness and wisdom. Students are expected to show the proper respect and accept whatever he dictates as the correct way to do things. There is no room for debate about his judgments. Even senior students who have trained with him for many years understand that he has the final word on any decision. This paternalism springs from traditional Japanese class structure, which demonstrated a strong Confucian influence, and is also reflective of the samurai ethos, which stressed loyalty above all else. Thus, the chief instructor of a dojo acts in a manner that suggests behavioral mores of the samurai leader in his relationship with his retainers. In a relationship similar to that of lord and samurai, the chief instructor of a modern Japanese dojo assigns rank to those who have trained long and have proven themselves loyal. They look to him for leadership and he in turn looks to them for support in teaching the junior members and performing whatever tasks are necessary around the dojo. (Western students sometimes have difficulty accepting this, but it is considered a privilege to be able to give instruction or perform other tasks that need be done for the instructor.)

Another part of this tradition that bears explanation is the *sempai-kohai* (lit., senior-junior) system. This system exists in many facets of Japanese society, from schools and colleges to fraternal organizations, as well as in the karate dojo. A *sempai* is simply one who is senior to his *kohai,* or junior, which means basically that the former has begun membership in the school, club, or other organization before the latter. Thus, in a karate dojo the *sempai* is usually a senior student who is responsible for assisting the new students in learning the correct etiquette and techniques. He may at times serve as assistant to the instructor and will take a particular interest in juniors who show an eagerness to learn. The *kohai* in turn should understand that his *sempai* is trying to help him and should therefore show him proper respect. This relationship between *sempai* and *kohai* is a life-long one and forms the basis for many relationships in other avenues of Japanese society. Entrance into the business world is usually much easier for a college graduate if he has a *sempai* among the employees of the company he wishes to join. In return, the *kohai* would support his *sempai* in future power struggles in the company and they could form a power block that would eventually benefit them both.

These rankings, once established, remain in effect throughout life. Even if one ceases to train or leaves the company, he is always thought of in reference to his place in the ranking order of seniors and juniors. This system is evident in numerous ways in the dojo and it may be observed in the class when students line up in order of rank to bow at the beginning and end of practice. During meetings of the higher ranking belts it is expected that the juniors will generally follow the lead of the seniors in discussions. Even the promotion system and awarding of belt grades is somewhat affected, since it is unusual to be promoted to a higher grade before one's *sempai*. In addition to the titles of *sempai* and *kohai,* the Japanese refer to their colleagues as *doryo*. This implies a sort of equality of rank or status; however, even among *doryo,* one may be graded according to time in the position.

A further element of Chinese philosophy adapted by the Japanese over the ages is the concept of the basic duality of the universe. Originally known in Chinese as *yin* and *yang,* the tradition holds that there are two opposing forces in the universe, positive and negative. The *yin* represents the negative, dark, female, passive, and weak forces, whereas the *yang* represents positive, bright, male, active, and strong forces. The standard *yin-yang* symbol is a

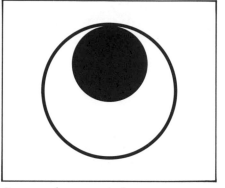

Chinese yin-yang symbol   Japanese in-yo symbol

circle divided by a curved line. This indicates that the two forces are inexorably intertwined within all things.

In Japanese this concept of duality is known as *in* and *yo,* and is represented by a dark circle inside a light one. The outside circle represents the universe, a large portion of which is shown as light *(yo)*. Within the large *yo* circle is shown a smaller circle *(in)* representing the opposing forces in the universe. Both are inseparable, as one is contained within the other.

The symbol for *in* and *yo* is used by many karate organizations in Japan, the most notable among them being the Japan Karate Association. Philosophically, it would be a good choice for most of the modern systems of Japanese karate since they all claim to be combinations of the two traditional schools of karate on Okinawa: the Shorin, which practiced light, flexible movements; and the Shorei, which emphasized strength in movement.

JUTSU AND DO

Various elements of bushido, the way of the warrior, have become part of the way of karate in Japan. The ideograph 武 *bu,* which stands for "martial" or "military," had long been viewed philosophically by the samurai, the class that it represented. Rather than seeing themselves primarily as military men or soldiers, *bushi* 武士, they chose to regard themselves as instruments of justice. To assert this claim, it was long popular among samurai and later among martial arts practitioners to offer a more peaceful rationalization for the character 武 *bu.* The explanation holds that the character is made up of two parts. The left side is the character 止, meaning "stop" or "prevent." The right side derives from the radical for spear 戈. It may also have been derived from an earlier Chinese character for dart or arrow 弋. The literal meaning of the combined characters is thus "to stop the spear." The right-hand part of the character carries with it the connotation of fighting, which then indicates that the true meaning of *bu* is "to stop the fight" or "to prevent the fight." A warrior could therefore view himself as an instrument of justice rather than as a hired killer.

The concept of the character is carried forth to the present day and fits in nicely with the view of martial arts as being a means of self-defense. Karate-do practitioners are quick to point out that the aim of karate training is to learn to protect onself, not to harm others. Thus the traditional explanation of the meaning of *bu* is still valid today.

There was, however, an obvious change in the basic philosophy of the fighting arts as Japan entered the present century. Originally designed to provide the most efficacious method of dispatching one's opponent, the arts of war were practiced in earnest through the early years of the Tokugawa rule. In those days, the possibility of actually facing an opponent with sword or spear was quite real, and training was aimed at giving the practitioner the greatest possible advantage. Techniques were not designed to impress onlookers or to demonstrate the grace and skill of the performer. Rather, the matter of self-preservation took precedence and the wielder of sword or spear was primarily concerned with sharpening skills that would do away with his antagonist with the greatest possible haste, since other opponents might be near. The classical arts of the sword, spear, empty hand, and bow and arrow all were practical in nature and were classed as "techniques," or *jutsu* 術. This label indicated that the form was utilitarian in purpose and its mastery was a matter of life and death. Thus, the traditional arts of kenjutsu, jujutsu, and others were practiced. By extension, we may consider the development of karate on Okinawa as a *jutsu* form (here called karate-jutsu) in that it was designed to kill one's opponent and was not practiced for any other reason.

In the later Tokugawa years, as the Meiji Restoration neared, it became increasingly obvious that the arts of ancient Japan were not practical in the more modern world. Numerous encounters with Western powers, notably the Perry expedition of 1853–54, left the Japanese with the realization that their weapons and techniques needed updating. (Hojutsu, the art of gunnery, had been practiced since the sixteenth century when the Japanese first obtained guns from European traders.) A scientific approach to war would be necessary. This led to a decline in the military value attached to the traditional arts that had so long been practiced in preparation for war.

With the advent of Western military practices, those arts of war native to Japan were kept alive by masters who sought ways to preserve their traditions in the modern world. The samurai had earlier used wooden swords, *bokken,* to test their skill against one another without actually risking loss of life. The *bokken* was crafted of oak and resembled a real sword in length, weight, and balance. In order to have a match with a *bokken,* the samurai would have to thrust or swing it at his opponent and stop just short of contact. This was considered a mark of skill, as one unused to the sword would not be able to control it in such a manner. In the eighteenth-century fencing master Chuto Nakanishi developed a split bamboo sword *(shinai)* and armor to be used in practice matches. The new invention gradually became popular in various schools of kenjutsu and in time became the basic equipment for the modern art of kendo, the descendent of kenjutsu.

In the word "kendo," the *do* 道 that followed *ken* 剣 indicated that the new art was the "way of the sword" as opposed to the old kenjutsu 剣術, "sword technique." Since the sword was no longer a practical weapon, the discipline required to master swordlike movements was considered the most important part of the art. The practitioner worked with the bamboo sword and armor in an attempt to perfect his character through rigid discipline and training. The most important part of the practice of kendo and other *do* arts is not the ability to dispatch one's opponent, but rather the process of mental and physical discipline that one undergoes in order to master the art, a view still held by present-day experts.

Karate did not arrive in Japan until the early twentieth century, by which time the national traditions of bushido had been firmly established. Since the way of the sword was the most important of the Japanese martial arts, it was only to be expected that the principles underlying the philosophy of kendo would have an influence on the practice and performance of the new martial art, karate. In a manner similar to the change from kenjutsu to kendo, karate-jutsu changed from a series of techniques designed to maim and kill an opponent into a system of mental and physical discipline, karate-do. Although the transition began in the nineteenth century on Okinawa, the influence of kendo on karate after the latter's introduction to Japan has been so great that the original Okinawan-Chinese blend of the art has become a form that may be called Japanese karate, which differs significantly in philosophy, if not performance, from the original. As with the transition in other Japanese fighting arts, karate-do eliminated some practice methods and aimed at a safer way of training, in which injuries would be kept to a minimum.

The practice of so-called *jutsu* arts may be labeled as "traditional." The *do* arts, such as karate-do, kendo, kyudo (archery), and judo are "traditionalistic."[1] That is to say, they are not an art that has been practiced for centuries in the same way, lasting to the present day. Rather, they follow the traditions that grew up with the traditional arts, but have been changed over the years. What we see in practice today is a latter-day relative of what were once extremely effective fighting systems. If these arts are traditionalistic, what of those who practice and teach them? Western students of the martial arts tend to view their kendo or karate-do instructors as men who are in no way different from the military men of the sixteenth century. In that respect they are in error. The man giving instructions with the wooden sword never went to war with a live blade in his hand, and has not had to rely upon it to preserve his life. Nor has the present-day karate master had to make great use of his art. In fact, the art of karate emphasizes the philosophy of *karate ni sente nashi,* or "no first attack." Students are told to avoid fights and to escape if at all possible. Only in extreme cases is the art of karate-do to be used against an actual opponent, and even then with great restraint.

The modern day "arts of war" are not really what they seem to be. It may be claimed that the practitioner of judo, karate-do, or aikido is ideally skilled in the arts of self-defense and well able to emerge victorious in an encounter with those less skillful. That is true; however, the key to understanding lies in the term "self-defense," which, as far as the art of karate do is concerned, is the key element. The art aims at the protection of oneself, and not the harming of others. If that facet is recognized, it will be easier to understand the difference between *jutsu* and *do*.

THE DOJO KUN

On the wall of virtually all karate training halls in Japan hangs a set of precepts known as the "Dojo Kun," said to have originated with an Okinawan karate master known as Karate Sakugawa (1733–1815). They state the following maxims: (1) seek perfection of character, (2) be faithful, (3) endeavor, (4) respect others, and (5) refrain from violent behavior. According to karate tradition they are the rules by which a *karate-ka* is supposed to live.

The first, "seek perfection of character," indicates that the art is more than just physical. Through rigorous training, the spirit to fight and succeed will be developed. Along with this fierce competitive spirit should come the realization that one's strength is great, and to use it and karate against the un-

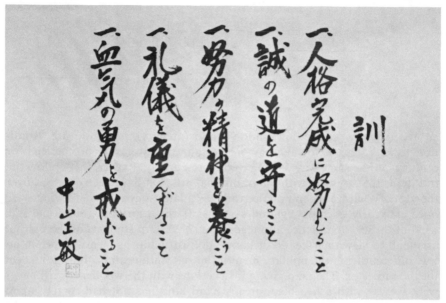

The Dojo Kun
Calligraphy by Masatoshi Nakayama, presented to Teruyuki Okazaki.

initiated is unfair. The practitioner should seek to subdue his mind as well as conquer the intricacies of body movement. Forging the spirit in the face of adversity will provide lifetime benefits. Even in old age when the body is no longer able to perform as well, the spirit can continue to grow.

To "be faithful" evidences a strong samurai tradition and by extension a Confucianist strain in the martial arts. In this sense, the faith to be shown is faith in one's instructors and seniors. The student must always be faithful to them and follow in much the same way as a medieval samurai was bound to follow his feudal lord. While this may seem unusual in the present day, it is unreasonable to expect an instructor to extend himself fully and teach all he knows to one who is likely to leave for the slightest reason. The faith extended to the instructor will be rewarded in that a greater amount of knowledge will be transmitted to the student. This bond between teacher and student is extremely valuable and is the basis of the learning relationship.

The "endeavor" mentioned in the Dojo Kun refers to the complete dedication to the effort necessary to achieve mastery of the martial art. In no case is mastery possible without strenuous effort on the part of the practitioner. This endeavor must be of a sincere nature and not just superficial. Serious endeavor on the part of the student will be recognized by the instructor, who will in turn spend more time with him.

Respect for others is common to the Japanese fighting systems in particular. It is frequently said that the martial arts begin and end with etiquette.

This is a reflection of the formal nature of the Japanese people and may be observed in the manner in which they conduct themselves in training sessions and generally in the presence of one another. Dojo etiquette is particularly well defined, requiring that all who enter the training hall pause and bow to the memory of past masters, usually memorialized in photographs or paintings in the front of the practice area. Prior to the beginning of class, students and instructors line up before the photographs, kneel, and meditate. They bow to the memory of past masters and then to one another from the kneeling position. This courtesy continues throughout the training session. Whenever an exercise, drill, or kata that uses two people or more is performed, it always begins and ends with a bow. Additionally, the bowing ceremony is repeated at the end of training after a closing period of meditation.

It is the responsibility of all trained practioners to "refrain from violent behavior" since a trained fighter can inflict serious injury upon others. The goal of karate training is self-mastery, including mastery of one's behavior. In situations where it is necessary to defend oneself, no non-violent alternative may be possible. However, the tradition handed down by great teachers indicates that after a life of training, they felt that they had failed if they were forced to resort to violent action against their fellow man, no matter how justified such actions might have been.

In the present day, refraining from violence is hard to explain to Westerners. Many people take up the art of karate with the purpose in mind of hurting others and they wish to learn how to do so as quickly as possible. It is therefore necessary for instructors to remember the Dojo Kun and to impress it upon their students. The Japan Karate Association has shortened the Dojo Kun and labeled it as their five guiding maxims. In abbreviated form they are character, sincerity, effort, etiquette, and self-control.

MARTIAL ARTS SAYINGS

The literature and lore of the martial arts is replete with sayings designed to foster contemplative thought among practitioners. The essence of the philosophy of the arts is passed on to the believers, who, if they understand the principle, will be able to master the technique. Most of these adages reflect a strong Zen influence: indeed, many of them are mentioned in the writings of Buddhist philosophers or are attributed to them. Presented below are a number of the more popular sayings and an explanation of their meanings.

1. *Ri no shugyo, waza no shugyo*　理の修行　わざの修行
(The study of reason and the study of technique)

This adage was discussed by the Zen priest Takuan in his letter of advice to the famed swordsman Yagyu Munenori in the seventeenth century. Munenori had requested that the priest instruct him in the uses of Zen in the fighting art. The response included a number of sayings and their explanations.

The *ri,* or reason, alluded to by Takuan is the total control of the mind that follows its detachment from worldly matters. This may also be described as the state of being "consciously unconscious" or "unconsciously conscious." In such a state, the mind is free to respond to whatever stimuli is presented to it. In the case of a swordsman facing his opponent or a *karate-ka* facing an assailant, it is necessary to free the mind of all thoughts of victory or defeat. Such concerns will inhibit the performance of the techniques that have been assiduously mastered and will ultimately lead to defeat. However, the mastery of the philosophy of *ri* is not the only guarantee of victory; it must be coupled with the mastery of *waza* or technique. In the mind of the master, the study of both is essential, and the study of either alone will not result in complete mastery.

2. *Kan ni hatsu o irezu*　間に髪を容れず
(Not room for even a single strand of hair)

The above is another adage discussed by Takuan. It emphasizes the necessity for spontaneous action generated by an uncluttered mind. Takuan noted that when one claps his hands, the sound that is produced is instantaneous; there is no gap between the action and the sound. In like manner, the practitioner in his response to an attack must be so "connected" that no gap is possible between the attack and his defense. If there is any hesitation between them, even enough "room for a single strand of hair," the gap will ultimately lead to defeat. When no gap exists, the attacker and defender become one and there is no chance for defeat. Such instantaneous response requires the mastery of both *ri* and *waza.*

3. *Sekka no ki*　石火の機
(The occasion of flint stones producing sparks)

This saying alludes to the process by which a spark is produced when two flint stones are struck together. Since this is a rapid movement and the result instantaneous, it indicates to the practitioner the freedom with which his mind must act. Movement in a fighting art is by necessity rapid, even though the mind that generates it remains at the same level of speed. That is to say, the rapid generation of the technique does not require the rapid movement of the mind; on the contrary, the mind is kept free and uncluttered and moves at a constant speed, unhindered by outside stimuli. The technique generated is the same in each instance.

4. *Mushin no kokoro* 無心の心
(Detached mind)

Mushin no kokoro is what all martial artists must strive for. This saying refers to a mind free to respond to any external stimuli, allowing free expression of any response technique. Another way to describe this state is to liken it to a mind empty of all thought or emotion, the presence of which interferes with the body's ability to act automatically in the face of an attack. A karate fighter facing his opponent in the ring is subject to the full range of human emotions, from fear to rage. His mind may be filled with thoughts of attack or defense, or reading his opponent's movements or intent. This state of mind is what Takuan described as "cluttered." By contrast, the detached mind does not stop at any one point. It is free to move about, allowing a flexibility to respond to any situation. This is the type of mind that a martial artist must strive for if he is to master the essence of the art.

5. *Mizu no kokoro* 水の心
(A mind like water)

Another description of the detached mind is the saying *mizu no kokoro*. This concept refers to a mind calm and clear like the surface of a pool of water. Such a surface acts as a mirror and reflects all that comes within its range. A martial artist who has trained his mind to be clear will find that it reflects instantaneously the actions of his opponent and allows an immediate response to an attack. A mind that is troubled by thoughts of attack and defense is like a pool whose surface is rippled by a breeze. Such a mind does not reflect and is useless in responding to an attack. Accordingly, the mind must be kept clear of thought in order to respond quickly.

6. *Tsuki no kokoro* 月の心
(A mind like the moon)

This is another attempt to describe the detached or unobstructed mind. The moon on a clear night reflects the light given off by the sun and is thus easily seen on the earth. However, at times the clear light of the moon is obstructed by clouds, giving an impression similar to that of a pond whose reflection is obscured by ripples. In this sense the clouds represent thoughts which freeze and focus the mind, making it unable to respond freely to the stimuli presented.

7. *Gi shin fuki* 技心不岐
(Technique and the mind are inseparable)

The Zen Buddhist influence of this saying is apparent. Rather than viewing the physical and mental aspects of martial arts as different, they are considered to be the same. The mind controls the body, and without the necessary control of the mind there can be no spontaneous technique, such as a reaction to an attack. Furthermore, the mind and technique must be equally developed in order to insure maximum efficiency in fighting. The practitioner who trains exclusively on physical technique without developing control over his mind will be limited. In like manner, great insights into the philosophy of fighting will be worthless if insufficient practice is conducted. The body will be unable to carry out the designs and strategy of the mind.

A further aspect of this saying is the instantaneous link between thought and action that is produced by strenuous, dedicated practice of the martial arts. From the viewpoint of Zen, the techniques generated by the mind are so closely connected that it is impossible to separate them.

8. *Ken shin fuki* 拳心不岐
(The fist and the mind are inseparable)

A variation of the previous saying, "technique and mind are inseparable," is "the fist and mind are inseparable." The two mean basically the same thing, except that in the former, the technique refers to all martial arts, while the latter specifically refers to karate.

9. *Do mu kyoku*　道無極
(No limitation for life)

Perhaps more than any other saying, this mirrors the essence of karate-do training. Even though human beings have physical limitations which may be reached in middle age, the mind and spirit can continue to make progress. Thus, the practitioner of the *do* forms of martial arts sees his art as an endeavor that may be continued throughout life. Mere physical proficiency in an art is not seen as a great accomplishment. Those who continue to train after their body has reached its physical limits are seen as the true masters of a *do*.

10. *Karate ni sente nashi*　空手に先手なし
(In karate there is no first attack)

This philosophy of karate has been handed down to the present day and has two basic elements. First, it indicates that the art of karate is designed for defense and not aggression. Second, it implies to the more advanced karate practitioner the wisdom of allowing his opponent to commit himself to an attack so that he may correctly respond with an effective counterattack. The practitioner must acquire the ability to read the opponent's moves as he begins them. To do this effectively, it is necessary to drill continuously in the basic movements of defense through the one-attack, three-attack, semi-free and free-style sparring drills (see Chapter 6). In such training one must watch the opponent closely and see how his body moves as he is about to execute each technique. In an actual fight the beginning postures or movements of a technique may be read just as the technique of attack is fully developed.

Evidence of this philosophy is apparent to even the casual observer of a karate training session, where sparring drills that emphasize the defensive moves are numerous and practiced with great frequency. For instance, in semi-free sparring, the defensive and offensive sides move about freely, the defense waiting for his opponent to initiate an attack. Once an aggressive movement has been initiated, there is no requirement for the defense to wait for its completion to counter. Indeed, if the beginning of the attack can be perceived, the defense may step in, jam it, and simultaneously counter. In not making the first move a successful defense is achieved.

In the kata also it will be noted that all begin with a defensive posture and then a blocking technique. None begins with an offensive move, it being assumed that the practitioner is training for self-defense and not for attack.

11. *Myo wa kyo-jitsu no kan ni ari*　妙在於虛實之間
(The essence lies between attack and defense)

This saying reflects the state of nothingness that may be seen as an escape from worldly things. In the case of a martial artist, these include fears of death and apprehension of all kinds experienced when facing an opponent. Thoughts of attack that race through the mind as one faces an opponent are thoughts that anchor the mind in one place. Thus fixed, it becomes impossible to move in free response to the opponent's moves. In like manner, thoughts of defense limit one to a set of movements anticipated on the part of the adversary. Somewhere between the two lies a middle ground where the mind floats freely and can respond instantaneously to external stimuli.

The problem of whether to attack or defend is answered by this saying. Continuous thoughts of attack are contrary to the philosophy of the martial arts, whose paramount goal is self-defense. Similarly, preoccupation with defense leads one to be timid in the face of an aggressor. Between them lies an area that is neither attack nor defense; this is the essence of the art.

12. *Koe naki o kiku, katachi naki o miru*　聽於無声　視於無形
(No-sound you can hear, no-image you can see)

"No-sound you can hear, no-image you can see" suggests a state of readiness for combat that indicates a high degree of development of a sixth sense. Through continuous training one may be able to discern that which is not evident to the untrained. Although faced with stimuli that the uninitiated might not respond to, the well-trained martial arts expert can readily pick up the slightest variation in his opponent's demeanor and interpret it through his training as an aggressive move. Through basic drills in sparring, this ability may be developed. In the sparring exercise, the perceptive trainee will not only practice how to avoid the attack and apply the proper block and counter, but will pay close attention to the initial stages of the attack that indicate its commencement. For example, untrained fighters may look at the area they are about to attack, tense their faces, twitch or make another sign that actually telegraphs the technique about to be executed. By having watched many opponents in training initiate the execution of a front kick or a stepping punch or any other aggressive movement, the master of karate has learned that a slight lean in one direction or a slight change in the position of the upper body indicates that a specific technique is about to begin. Having read his opponent's move prior to its inception, he is then in a position to counter before the opponent can get started.

This ability to see the unseeable and hear the unhearable is not as mystical as it might seem. It merely requires diligent observation through the course of numerous training sessions.

13. *Ikken hissatsu* 一拳必殺
(One-punch death-blow)

The concept of "one-punch death-blow" has been greatly misunderstood by American martial artists, particularly those who have not trained under Japanese instructors. Rather than placing all their strength in one technique as they perform sparring drills, they are more likely to counter an attack with a flurry of kicks and punches. If they had confidence in their ability to deliver a single, decisive blow, there would be no need for all these extras.

Those practicing the vigorous Japanese-Okinawan systems, though, have long understood the meaning of this saying and its relation to their training. In actuality, it is combat-oriented and presupposes a life-and-death situation. To illustrate this, imagine a karate practitioner in a situation where he is attacked by several assailants, each of whom is armed or otherwise capable of rendering him hors de combat. In all likelihood, one chance is all that he will have to parry an attack by one assailant and deliver a vital blow, since if he misses, the assailant will continue the attack or the other assailants may close in. The blow delivered must injure the attacker to the point where he is rendered harmless. Extreme concentration of force must be used with the realization that there is only one opportunity. The technique must be delivered with no thought of a follow-up, for to do otherwise would make survival questionable.

This idea is reflected in training methods, particularly in the basic techniques of three-attack, one-attack, and semi-free sparring. In the latter two especially, only one punch or kick and one block and counterattack are permitted. No follow-up techniques are allowed.

Ikken hissatsu is further emphasized in the examinations for high-colored belts and the first-degree black belts (see Appendix). Those who take these exams must demonstrate that they have confidence that their one punch or kick can disable an opponent. A point is counted against an examinee when he follows his initial counter-attack with other punches or kicks. This indicates to the examiner that he is not sure of the strength or effectiveness of his first counter.

14. *Shu ha ri* 守破離
(Obedience, divergence, transcendence)

The process through which one masters a martial art is divided into three stages. They are *shu* 守, obedience to tradition; *ha* 破, breaking away from tradition; and *ri* 離, transcending tradition. (It may be noted that this process applies as well to other Zen-oriented Japanese arts such as flower arrangement and the tea ceremony.)

The beginning of martial arts practice involves study under a teacher who has mastered the art and fully understands the process by which learning takes place. Usually the student has little knowledge of the art. In order to arrive at the desired goal, it is necessary to begin by learning the basic techniques. This involves a great deal of physical effort on the part of the student, as he must approximate the movements taught with as little deviation from the norm as possible. The student is not free to interpret, and must strive to emulate that which is described as the perfect stance, step, or block. In the study of karate, this stage of rigid obedience to the standard lasts up to the rank of Shodan, or first-degree black belt.

Once the basic movements of the martial art have been mastered, the practitioner must then make certain changes in them. That is to say, they must be adapted to his own body type. Those who are large and powerful may emphasize techniques that ultilize strength, while those who are light may practice differently so that they will have the ability to shift and evade an assailant. In addition to emphasizing certain techniques, they may also alter to a certain degree the manner in which a movement is performed. In diverging, the practitioner must individualize the basic techniques of his art until he makes his own fighting style. Thus, between Shodan and Sandan (third-degree black belt), the style of fighting will have begun to change from the commonly accepted standard. Those who pass the Sandan test will have demonstrated this divergence, or *ha*. From an examiner's point of view, several black belts taking the Sandan exam will all move and fight differently.

The third and final stage in the mastery of a martial art is *ri*, or transcendence. This implies that the practioner has passed beyond technique and fully understands its philosophy. Those who have achieved this level of understanding are few in number and are ranked from fourth to tenth degree; those of the fourth and fifth degree are usually passing from the divergent to the transcendent stage, while those of the sixth degree and above are considered to have reached it.

In general, the first stage of training, *shu,* takes from two to five years of regular training. The second stage, *ha,* is longer, usually spanning a period of from five to ten years. The final step, *ri,* involves another five to ten years of training, although the study of the art is continuous and progress never ceases as long as effort is made. The time span of the stages given here is approximate, since individuals differ in their intrinsic abilities, and the qualifications of their instructors will vary.

Little has been written about this concept, although it is well known to instructors, having been handed down over the centuries as part of the oral tradition of the Japanese martial arts. Said to date from the 1500s, it is believed to have Chinese origins. The concept of *shu ha ri* obviously has a strong Buddhist flavor.

15. *Ken zen itchi* 拳禅一致
(The fist and Zen are the same)

This is an interesting saying that reflects the Zen influence on the art of karate-do. Karate on Okinawa never had a strong Buddhist feeling in the same way that the Japanese arts of the sword and bow did; rather, the Zen tradition became part of the essence of karate-do when it came to popularity in Japan proper.

The basic meaning of the saying is that karate training is like the practice of Zen in that it must be experienced in order to be fully understood. In some sects of Buddhism, particularly Zen, verbal explanations and logic are the least useful in explaining the nature of things. In like manner, traditional karate instructors never gave lengthy explanations of the rationale behind training or a particular technique. Rather, through great repetition, the student would gradually gain insight into the meaning of movements and come to an understanding on his own. As in Zen, there is a major emphasis on the direct transmission of knowledge from master to student and in that sense there is great similarity in the practice of Zen and karate-do.

The sayings mentioned above are only some of many that went hand in hand with traditional Japanese fighting arts. Their continued use by karate practitioners today gives evidence to the fact that these traditional arts have had an effect on present day karate-do.

Ken zen itchi (The fist and Zen are the same)
Calligraphy by Masatoshi Nakayama, presented to the Kobukan Karate Club, Toms River, New Jersey.

PART TWO | Karate Training

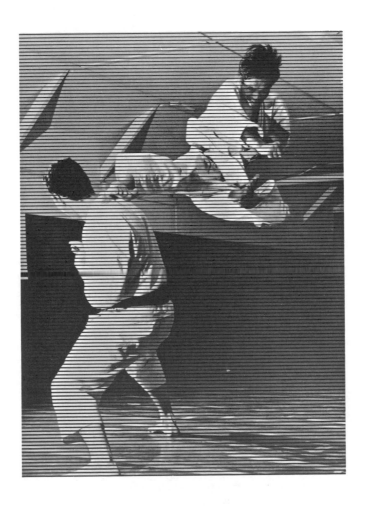

(Overleaf) **A** jumping side thrust-kick demonstrated by
Shojiro Koyama, Japan Karate Association instructor.

5

Preparation and Etiquette

In discussing karate as self-defense, it is important to bear in mind that the essence of karate is just that, self-defense. Beginning students are usually given valuable lectures by their instructors as to the meaning of karate, and it is emphasized that the art is to be used to protect oneself rather than to harm others. This philosophy is further reinforced as the student progresses to learning the formal exercises, or kata. Each kata begins with a defensive technique, rather than a position of attack. It may be seen by the casual observer, as well as the practitioner, that the nature of karate is defensive rather than offensive.

Serious self-defense begins with advance preparation, both physical and mental. The physical side of self-defense obviously involves training the body to the state where it may respond to an attack with strong defensive movements and counterattacks if necessary. The mental side of karate training for self-defense involves two aspects: the preparation of the mind, and the practice of common sense. The concept of *mushin,* or "no-mindedness," was discussed in Chapter 2 (p. 65); suffice to say here that it applies to self-defense situations in the same way it applies to any situation where the martial arts must be used. The mind must be controlled to the extent that it does not interfere with the reflexive actions of the body that have been learned through arduous training. The practice of kata are pertinent here as well in that by helping the practitioner to concentrate on imaginary opponents and to meet a series of attacks from all directions, they combine the physical and mental aspects of self-defense.

The second aspect of the mental side of self-defense involves the use of common sense. This may be more difficult to achieve for some than others, since it is generally conceded that one is born with common sense and it is difficult to acquire otherwise. However, there is no reason why one cannot, through experience, learn that there are certain situations that may be avoided. We can all understand that a trip through the bad section of town in the late hours is an invitation to attack. But there are more subtle circumstances that may also lead to trouble, for example, discussing controversial topics with

1

strangers or slight acquaintances. Perhaps the worst situation of all is to have to defend oneself against an acquaintance, since there would be a great deal of reluctance to use deadly techniques against such a person. The best self-defense is one which does not involve any fighting technique at all. In short, avoidance, talking one's way out, or just leaving when danger seems imminent, is the preferred course of action.

THE STANDING BOW

The fourth admonition of the Dojo Kun, or rules for training in the dojo, is to respect others. As referred to by the Japan Karate Association, it is known as etiquette. Consequently, all the sparring drills that follow begin and end with the opponents bowing to one another. This indicates that there is mutual respect and that the participants will stop their techniques short of contact so as not to cause injury to their training partners.

The correct manner for performing the standing bow is illustrated in Figures 1 to 3. Both sides bow at the same time. The body is inclined forward from the waist about 30 degrees, the eyes fixed on the opponent's body. Bowing too low will not allow one to see the opponent, which is an invitation to an attack, while bowing at too slight an angle, just nodding the head, or looking at the opponent's face while bowing are considered disrespectful.

2

3

THE KNEELING BOW

The kneeling bow is performed by the instructor and his students before and after the actual training session. It is also performed by two practitioners who are training in defensive techniques from a kneeling position.

The correct way of bowing is very old and reflects a strong samurai tradition, since the manner of the bow was determined by the necessities of self-defense. In traditional Japan, the badge of the samurai was the wearing of two swords, a custom that denoted his rank in society. Since he was ostensibly ready to use the swords at all times, it was necessary to remain in a position to do so, even when bowing. Thus, the placement of the knees and the position of the body when bowing were aimed at allowing him the maximum ability to defend himself as he performed the courtesy.

4

5

4¹ (wrong)

5¹ (wrong)

6

7

The traditional bow began by placing the left knee on the floor first. In this manner the sword could be drawn easily. If the right knee were placed down first it would be difficult to draw the sword smoothly (Figs. 4, 5). Once the left knee and then the right were on the floor, the performer would then sit back on his feet, with either his left foot crossed over his right or his left big toe crossed on top of his right big toe (Figs. 6, 7).

8   9   10

11   12   13

To perform the modern bow, lower yourself to the floor as described above. Place the left hand on the floor first and then the right. This is done because the right hand would be kept free until the last moment to grasp the sword, which was placed on the floor to the left of the person bowing. When actually bowing, look forward to the lower part of the opponent's body (to prevent a surprise attack). Raise the right (sword) hand from the floor first. Advance the right knee and stand up.

Figures 8 to 17 show the correct sequence for the modern kneeling bow.

14

15

16

17

6

Kumite: Sparring Techniques

For our purposes, the term "kumite" is used to describe a variety of karate training drills designed to give the practitioner experience in using diverse techniques against an actual opponent. Some of these drills may be prearranged and some may be spontaneous. As the purpose of each drill is different, the rationale behind the drills varies according to the situation.

ELEMENTS OF FIGHTING

The general purpose of sparring is the practice of the basic elements of fighting: distancing, timing, perception of attack, acceleration, balance, technique, and focus. In order to better understand the modes of training, it is necessary to expand upon the preceeding terms.

Distancing: Maintaining the proper distance between yourself and your opponent is very important. In beginning the attack or responding with a counterattack after blocking the opponent's initial attack, it is vital that the practitioner be neither too close nor too far from his adversary. If too close, the technique may lack strength or be jammed. Even if delivered correctly, it will still not be strong, as a longer technique is generally more powerful. The opposite fault would be to distance oneself too far away. This would result in missing the opponent completely or in delivering a blow at the fullest extension of the arm or leg, causing a significant loss of power.

Timing: This element of fighting involves the delivery of a blow to the opponent's body at exactly the correct moment, for maximum effect. If the blow is delivered too soon, the opponent may not yet be at the correct distance and the blow will miss or not have enough power. If too late, the attack may be blocked or jammed. Timing is also used to throw an opponent off guard so that a blow may be delivered with greater efficiency. Aiming a punch at the midsection as the opponent's arm is rising to block a first punch to the face, for example, would utilize the best elements of timing technique.

Perception of Attack: This requires concentration. Through careful observation of many different opponents it is possible to read their movements.

Less skilled attackers will usually "telegraph" their attacks by indicative motions of the hand, hips, upper torso, or head. With training, however, these indicators of attack become more subtle and require greater expertise to foresee. Continuous practice in watching the attack will develop one's ability to perceive an attack.

Acceleration: This is an extremely important part of technique. It involves moving one's body from a stationary position to one of attack or defense with the greatest possible speed. It is especially useful when launching an attack, as it gives the attacker the advantage over his opponent if his acceleration is quick enough to escape the perception of his enemy.

Balance: All techniques must be performed in a balanced position. The results of bad balance are poor timing, loss of power in technique, and vulnerability to attack.

Technique: The techniques applied in the practice of sparring must be smooth and efficient. They must also be relevant to the other elements of fighting; for example, the close punch must be used if the distance is limited, and kicking techniques may be called for if the opponent is out of range of hand techniques. On more advanced levels, this also refers to the style of fighting applied to the opponent. One usually must fight different opponents with different methods. What is efficient and workable against a 140-pound man may be impossible against one weighing 220 pounds.

Focus: This refers to the instantaneous concentration of all physical and mental energy at the point of impact. Since correct focus lasts only for a split second, perfect timing and coordination of all muscle groups must take place. Usually the larger and slower muscle groups, such as the hips and trunk, are moved first, and the muscles of the hand and arm follow so that all will tense in the correct position upon impact.

TYPES OF DRILLS

Prearranged Drills

SINGLE-ASSAILANT MULTIPLE-STEP: The most common of these are three- and five-attack sparring drills, although seven-attack sparring drills may be used. The main purpose of such drills, aside from basic practice in technique, is to find the correct distance in relation to the opponent. The defender must judge and adjust the distance between himself and his opponent each time the latter steps forward. In the attack and counter, any of the basic techniques may be used, including all blocks, hand and leg attacks, and defensive moves. It is usual to have the lower grades work on these drills a great deal using the rising, forearm, and downward blocks, in conjunction with the counterpunch or front kick.

SINGLE-ASSAILANT SINGLE-STEP: In these drills, as in the multiple step drills, the attack is prearranged, the only difference being that one step is taken in the attack. It may also be practiced without prearranged targets, although this is not practical for low-graded students. The main purpose of this drill, aside from basic training in technique, is to reduce the reaction time between the block and counterattack. It also develops the ability to perceive the opponent's attack. A variation of this drill involves one step with two punches. The circle drill, included here as a multiple assailant drill, in which a ring of opponents consecutively attack a defender in the center, can be considered a complex single-step drill.

MULTIPLE ASSAILANT: The multiple-assailant drills differ from the preceding in that there may be many attackers against a single defender. In practice, this sort of training is difficult; however, it has the advantage of allowing the practitioner a certain degree of familiarity with the possibilities of defense when faced with numerous real adversaries. In this type of drill, the principle of *ikken hissatsu* is extremely important. Only by defeating each opponent with one technique may the defender hope to even the odds. If the one punch or kick is not fully effective, there may not be time for a second, since attackers are all around. Total concentration must be put into each technique.

SEMI-FREE SPARRING: These drills are usually practiced by advanced students. Both practitioners move around in a relaxed combative position as though they were actually fighting. Only a single attack and counter combination is used. Semi-free sparring develops the same skills as the single-assailant drills. However, it is more difficult, since both practitioners are free to move about and adjust the distance between them throughout the drill.

Free-Style Fighting

SLOW-MOTION SPARRING: This appears to be actual fighting as viewed through a slow motion camera. It involves an unlimited use of karate techniques and movement and allows for practice of combinations and experimentation. This type of training, as well as semi-free sparring, allows for the maximum amount of practice in all elements of sparring, including body shifting, distancing, and combinations of attacks and defensive movement.

FREE-STYLE SPARRING: This is perhaps the ultimate practice for advanced students. It involves actual full-speed fighting against an opponent. The purpose of this is to practice all elements of fighting, including the development of endurance, strategy, and fighting spirit.

Although a number of sparring drills and exercises have been mentioned, the list is by no means exhaustive. An imaginative instructor may develop variations or combinations of the above exercises to train certain individuals or to overcome general problems that his class is experiencing.

Finally, it should be noted that the prearranged kumite which follow should be practiced on both left and right sides, even though the instructions and photos show the drills from only one side.

PREARRANGED DRILLS

Single-Assailant Multiple-Step

■ THREE-ATTACK SPARRING DRILL

The three-attack sparring drill *(sambon kumite)* has training in distancing, stance, timing, blocking, and countering techniques as its basic objectives. It may be expanded from three steps to a five- or seven-step drill if space in the training hall permits.

The attacker assumes the downward blocking position in the front stance. The defender stands in the natural stance (Fig. 1). It is important to begin these sparring drills in the natural stance, since this is the position that one would likely be in if attacked. Thus, one must move from a normal, everyday position to defense.

The attacker steps in and performs a lunge punch to the face. The defender steps back and blocks with a rising block (Fig. 2). Again, the attacker steps in and punches to the face (Fig. 3). In all, three steps and lunge punches are performed and the defender steps back and uses the rising block for defense each time. After the defender blocks the third time, he counters with a reverse punch to the midsection (Figs. 4, 5). The counter may also be practiced with an attack to the upper or lower target areas.

Common Errors: As shown in Figure 5[1], the defender has retreated too far, so his opponent is out of range of his punch. In Figure 5[2] he has allowed the attacker to come in too close, making a shorter and weaker technique necessary.

2   3

4   5

5¹ (wrong)   5² (wrong)

11

12

13

14

Variations: (i) In addition to using the hands to attack in the three-attack sparring drill, one may also use the feet. Figures 6 to 10 show a series of attacks using the front snap-kick. The defender is using the downward block. It is also possible for the attacker to use the side thrust-kick or the roundhouse kick.

(ii) A kick may also be used in the counterattack at the end of the drill. Figures 11 and 12 show the defender after he has moved his front (left) foot back in order to adjust the distance between himself and his attacker. He then steps in and delivers a front snap-kick with his right foot. This is a particularly valuable training method in adjusting the kicking distance.

(iii) Figures 13 and 14 show another variation in the counterattack. The defender is using a knife-hand strike here.

15

(iv) As an overall variation on the basic three-attack sparring drill, a different type of move is used in each of the three attacks. In Figures 15 to 20 the first attack is to the face, the second to the midsection, and the third to the lower part of the body. All three attacks are lunge punches. The defender uses a rising block, an outside forearm- block, and a downward block, respectively. A front-snap kick is used instead of a punch for the counterattack.

In practice, any blocking and countering combination may be used, and some variation is encouraged in order to give students training in a wide variety of techniques.

Single-Assailant Single-Step

■ ONE-ATTACK SPARRING DRILL

The one-attack sparring drill *(ippon kumite)* is designed to give the defender practice in cutting down the time between the block and the counter. Through intensive practice in three- and five-attack sparring, stance and basic movements are developed. In this next higher form of training for free sparring, the reaction time must be perfected. One also begins to get the feeling for the principle of *ikken hissatsu,* or one punch with total force. Both the attacker and defender are allowed only one move each to attack the opponent; therefore, all force must be concentrated on the single blow.

It is not necessary to step directly back in this drill: the defender may step to the side or at any angle, as well as stepping forward to block the opponent's move at its inception.

16 17

18

19 20

21

22

23

Drill 1: The attacker steps in and performs a lunge punch to the face. The defender steps back and executes a rising block and then counters with a reverse punch to the midsection (Figs. 21–23).

Drill 2: The attacker steps in and performs a lunge punch to the midsection. The defender shifts to the outside and performs a knife-hand block in the back stance. The defender follows with a front kick to the midsection using the forward leg (Figs. 24–26).

Drill 3: The attacker performs a front kick to the midsection. The defender uses a low sweeping block and counters with a roundhouse kick to the solar plexus (Figs. 27–29).

24

25

26

27

28

29

30

31

32

33

34

35

36

37

38

Drill 4: The attacker performs a roundhouse kick to the head. The defender shifts to the right and blocks with an inside forearm-block. He then performs a counterpunch to the face (Figs. 30–32).

Drill 5: The attacker steps in and performs a lunge punch to the face. The defender uses an outside forearm-block and then shifts into the straddle stance and counters with an elbow thrust to the ribs (Figs. 33–35).

■ ONE-ATTACK DRILL WITH MULTIPLE COUNTERS

This type of drill is best practiced by more advanced students, since the student must focus more than one counterattack. An inexperienced trainee will usually forget to focus the first counterattack, but will concentrate only on the second.

Drill 1: The attacker steps in and performs a lunge punch to the face. The defender blocks with an extended knife-hand block and counters simultaneously with a side snap-kick to the ribs. He then follows up with a roundhouse kick to the kidneys (Figs. 36–38).

39   40

41   42

Drill 2: The attacker steps in and performs a lunge punch to the face. The defender uses a backhand block and then counters with a roundhouse kick to the neck. He follows through with a rising elbow-strike to the chin (Figs. 39–42).

Drill 3: The attacker steps in and performs a lunge punch to the midsection. The defender shifts to the outside and uses a knife-hand block in the back stance. He then performs a front kick to the ribs using his front leg and follows through with a reverse punch (Figs. 43–46).

Drill 4: The attacker steps in and performs a lunge punch to the lower midsection. The defender uses a downward block. He then shifts his front foot back to adjust space for a front kick with the rear foot to the midsection, and follows with a lunge punch to the face (Figs. 47–51).

43

44

45

46

47

48

49

50

51

■ ONE-STEP TWO-ATTACK SPARRING DRILL

The drills to this point have been concerned with the blocking and countering of a single attack. In this drill the attacker has two opportunities to attack and the defender must block both of these prior to delivering a counterblow.

Drill 1: The attacker steps in and performs a right lunge punch to the face and then a left reverse punch to the midsection. The defender blocks these with his left hand, performing a rising block and an outside forearm-block, respectively. He then counters with a right reverse punch to the solar plexus (Figs. 52–55).

52

53

54

55

56

57

58

59

Drill 2: (This variation actually involves two steps.) The attacker steps in and performs a left lunge punch to the face. The defender steps back with his left foot and uses a right rising block. The attacker then executes a right front kick and lands. The defender steps to the right rear by shifting his right foot and blocks using a left downward block. He counters with a right reverse punch to the solar plexus (Figs. 56–59).

Remember to practice these drills on both left and right sides.

60

61

62

63

■ DIRECTION-REVERSING DRILL

In this form of sparring, the attacker steps forward and delivers a blow while the defender steps back and blocks as usual. The defender then advances to counter the attacker, who blocks and delivers a counterattack.

Drill 1: The attacker steps in and executes a lunge punch to the face while the defender performs a rising block. The defender then steps in with a punch to the midsection while the attacker blocks with an outside forearm-block and counters with a counterpunch to the midsection (Figs. 60–63).

64

65

66

67

Drill 2: The first attack is a lunge punch to the midsection, defended by an outside forearm-block. The defender's move is a lunge punch to the face, countered by a rising block. The attacker then counterpunches to the midsection (Figs. 64–67).

124 · PART TWO: KARATE TRAINING

68

69

Multiple Assailant

■ THREE-MAN DRILL

The first of these exercises involves defense against two assailants. In the accompanying illustrations they are positioned in front and in back of the defender. Other variations would include placing them on either side, or on one side and behind. The defender must make sure that his move against the attacker in the front is effective, or as he turns to meet the attacker in the rear, he will be open to further attack from the first assailant.

Drill 1: The defender blocks an attack to the face using a rising block, and counters with a punch to the midsection. He then turns and blocks using the vertical knife-hand. This is followed by a counterpunch to the midsection (Figs. 68–73).

70

71

72

73

74

75

76

Drill 2: The defender uses a backhand block and then counters with a roundhouse kick to the first opponent's midsection. Without putting his foot down, he immediately executes a back thrust-kick to stop the attack from the rear. As the kick is completed, he turns to the rear and sweeps the second opponent's attacking hand aside with a vertical knife-hand block, and counter-punches to the midsection (Figs. 74–80).

77

78

79
80

81

82

■ CIRCLE DRILL

In the circle drill the defender, again, has only one chance to defeat each attacker, so the single punch or kick must be powerful.

The defender stands in the center of a circle of attackers, in the ready position. The attackers all assume the downward block *(gedan-barai)* position. The elementary way to practice is to have the attackers in succession perform one lunge punch to the defender's head as the attack moves either clockwise or counterclockwise. The defender must continually shift to meet the new attack. As each attacker is countered, he shifts back to the ready position and the next attacker in the circle executes his attack.

Variations of this include allowing each attacker to execute any attack, or assigning each attacker a number, which the instructor calls out at random. The latter variation requires that the defender be ready for an attack from any direction.

In the drill shown in Figures 81 to 92 the attack is moving in a counterclockwise direction, and the attackers are all delivering a lunge punch to the defender's head. The defender is countering with various kicks and punches.

83

84

85

86

87

88

89

90

91

92

93 94

95 96

■ DOUBLE-LINE DRILL

In this advanced form of sparring drill, the emphasis is on defending oneself from surprise attack. The defender must walk between two lines of attackers, who launch attacks at him one after another. The attacks may be predetermined or at the attacker's choice, depending on the skill of the defender.

To begin, both lines of attackers assume the downward block position. The defender begins to walk down the line. The first attacker on his right steps forward and attacks; the defender blocks and counters appropriately. After the attacker steps back to his original position in the line, the defender blocks and counters an attack from the first attacker on his left. The defender continues down the line, countering attacks alternately from the right and left (Figs. 93–113).

132 · PART TWO: KARATE TRAINING

97

98

99

100

101

102

103

104

105

106

107

108

109

110

111

112

113

114

115

116

■ SINGLE-LINE DRILL

In this drill the defender assumes the front stance with his back to the wall. He must then block and counter a series of single attacks. As each attacker steps in and performs a predetermined attack, the defender blocks and counters. The attacker then goes to the end of the line and the attacks are continued.

In the illustrations here, the attacks are all to the face and the defender counters with a variety of moves (Figs. 114–126).

117

118

119

120

121

122

123

124

125

126

127

Semi-Free Sparring

Semi-free sparring *(jiyu ippon kumite)* is the means by which advanced players sharpen their technique. In this type of prearranged sparring, only the attack and target area are predetermined, usually by the attacker calling them out himself. Normally, attacks include lunge punches to various areas, and front and side kicks. Both players move about in a relaxed free stance and are allowed to feint and body shift in order to throw off the opponent's timing. Only a single attack is allowed, so the attacker must focus upon the mastering of "one-punch death-blow." When the attacker is able to score even after announcing his move, it can be said that he has truly mastered the technique. Such mastery takes years of practice.

Four possible sparring sequences are illustrated here. It should be noted that there will likely be more free movement than can be shown in a few photographs. Remember to begin each drill with a bow.

Drill 1: The attacker has announced a right lunge punch to the face. When this is accomplished, the defender counters, here with a counterpunch to the midsection (Figs. 127–129).

Drill 2: The attacker has announced a right front snap-kick to the lower part of the body. The defender counters with a counterpunch to the body (Figs. 130–132).

128

129

130

131

132

133

134

135

Drill 3: The attacker has announced a right lunge punch to the midsection. The defender counters with a left outside forearm-block and a right counterpunch to the midsection (Figs. 133–135).

Drill 4: The attacker has announced a right side thrust-kick to the upper body. The defender blocks with a left outside forearm-block and counters with a right counterpunch to the midsection (Figs. 136–138).

142 · PART TWO: KARATE TRAINING

136

137

138

FREE-STYLE FIGHTING

Free-style fighting *(jiyu kumite)* may be practiced either at full or half speed, or in slow motion. If practiced in slow motion, the emphasis should be on developing smooth body movement; thus, no real strength should be put into the moves. When done in slow motion or half speed, the players usually remain at ease and try to improve their technique.

139   140

When practiced at full speed, there is usually an emphasis on the scoring of points or on the speedy combination of techniques. All techniques of offense must be stopped short of contact, and a few dangerous techniques, such as attacks to the groin, eye, and knee, are prohibited. The position for free sparring should be a relaxed one in which the body is able to move in all directions; thus, an extremely low stance is not particularly useful, since it cuts mobility. The skillful fighter shifts into such low stances from the higher sparring stance during the performance of techniques and then shifts rapidly out in order to keep mobility.

Figures 139 and 140 show two stances, or *kamae,* for free fighting showing individual fighting attitudes.

7

Karate Kata

The kata is a unique exercise that encompasses the very essence of a martial art. A kata, or form, is by definition a predetermined set of movements that represents the motions of blocking, striking, punching, and kicking against imaginary opponents. In the history of virtually all Japanese martial arts, kata have been an invaluable part of training. The kata of karate, moreover, are of Okinawan or even Chinese origin.

BACKGROUND AND APPLICATIONS

In order to appreciate fully what a kata is, one must bear in mind that it represents a condensation of knowledge. The master who devised the form, drawing from his experience, put together a set of movements, usually less than forty or fifty in number. As one practices these movements, the wealth of information that has been put into the particular kata gradually begins to reveal itself. The process of the creation of a kata and its being passed on is shown below.

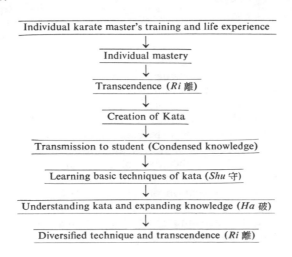

Individual karate master's training and life experience
↓
Individual mastery
↓
Transcendence (*Ri* 離)
↓
Creation of Kata
↓
Transmission to student (Condensed knowledge)
↓
Learning basic techniques of kata (*Shu* 守)
↓
Understanding kata and expanding knowledge (*Ha* 破)
↓
Diversified technique and transcendence (*Ri* 離)

1   2   3   4

5   6

To understand how the knowledge of past masters may be drawn out of these "living textbooks," let us examine a position common to several kata. The position shown in Figures 1–4, in which the right augmented fore-arm-block is performed from a stance in which the left foot is crossed behind the right, is the first move of the kata Bassai Dai (p. 191), and may also be found in slight variation in other forms. Illustrated in Figures 5 and 6 are two of the many possible applications of the technique. In Figure 5 the fighters show the move being used against a punching attack; in Figure 6 is shown a much older application of the movement, namely, jamming an opponent's hand down as he attempts to draw his sword.

An essential part of understanding any position in a kata is the realization of potential follow-up movements, which are not, of course, part of the kata

7   8

9

itself. To continue our example, once the block has been performed, what must then be done to insure that the opponent does not continue the attack? The number and variation of the movements that spring from any position are limited only by the performer's imagination. The longer the form is practiced, the more possibilities will be understood. Figures 7 and 8 show two simple follow-up movements. In Figure 7 the attacker has begun to retreat and the defender shifts forward and executes a right lunge punch to the face; in Figure 8 a counterpunch to the midsection is used. Either of these movements may be performed stepping toward the opponent or shifting back, depending on the situation.

Another possible follow-up move is shown in Figure 9. In this instance the attacker has retreated and the defender has twisted slightly to the side in order to execute a side thrust-kick.

10   11

12   13

A more complex counterattack involves a throw followed by a punch. From the crossed leg-blocking position, the right foot is advanced to the outside of the attacker's right leg. Simultaneously grasping the attacker's clothing and sweeping his leg out from under him, the defender then follows up with a punch to his downed assailant (Figs. 10–13).

It should be noted that although many such obvious applications of kata moves exist, there are also many moves and positions which are very old and whose applicability to combat is open to question since no data describing their combat effectiveness exists.

In present-day practice of karate in America there seems to be some dispute over the usefulness of kata. Those who have not trained under Japanese instructors or their students seem to feel that the kata is merely an art form, a kind of dancing. As a result there are schools that completely leave out the practice of kata in their daily training. Instead, they emphasize free fighting in preparation for tournaments. In truth, however, the practice of kata is essential to the development of self-defense techniques in a way that tournament-style free fighting can never be.

When karate entered the twentieth century, the masters practicing it knew that if it were to survive it would have to change with the times. As the twentieth century passed its first few decades, the pressure mounted to turn karate into sport and physical education. In time this was done. However, in order to make karate into a sport that would permit competition, it was necessary to eliminate what were considered dangerous techniques, such as attacks to the knee joint, groin, and eyes. The problem of how to train for self-defense and learn the older, combat-oriented movements thus arose. The answer lay in the kata. Since the older kata of both the Shorin and Shorei schools were devised in an era when there was no sport karate, they include numerous movements designed to dispatch an opponent quickly. A cursory examination of the kata Bassai Dai (p. 191) shows that there are strikes to the region of the groin, kicks to the knee joint, stomps to the top of the foot, and other techniques that would be prohibited in competition under present-day rules.

The key to learning karate as a self-defense system, then lies in mastery of the kata. We find interwoven throughout them numerous methods of thwarting an attack and finishing off an opponent who threatens one's life.

In practicing a kata, the following points are important:

1. Correct sequence: The movements themselves are predetermined as is their sequence. No deviation is allowed from this.

2. Embusen: This refers to a prearranged line of movement. The performer of the kata must follow this floor plan if the kata is to be done correctly.

3. Correct understanding: Each movement in the kata, whether offensive or defensive, has a meaning. The performer must show that he understands the rationale of each through his performance.

4. Application: As each move has a meaning, one must learn all the possibilities from each position. This is the hidden meaning of the form and is not readily understandable to the casual observer.

5. Rhythm: The rhythm of fighting is varied; it is sometimes fast, sometimes slow. Techniques are grouped, punctuated by pauses, continued, and combined. Thus, the rhythm of kata must follow that of actual combat. Each kata has its own particular rhythm that the performer must master in order to demonstrate its relationship to combat. Rhythm includes timing, focus, and, smooth flexible movement.

6. Breathing: The conclusion of each movement usually coincides with exhalation, while the preparatory positions and movements are ones during which the performer inhales. Knowing how to do this is an important part of the kata. One must also give a *kiai,* or shout, and tense at the correct moment in each kata. In most, there are two moves that call for a *kiai.*

7. Correct positioning of the body parts: This is especially important in the case of hand techniques, as a little variation in the position may render the form incorrect.

KATA NAMES AND ORIGINS

The two traditional schools of karate on Okinawa developed separately and in secret due to the oppressive practices of the Japanese who ruled there. Thus, different methods of fighting and training were used in each. The kata of the Shorin school emphasized light, flexible movements, while those of the Shorei school used strong, powerful movements. The kata were assigned names, often of the originator, but more commonly names that indicated something about the kata itself and the style of fighting it effected.

After its introduction to Japan in the twentieth century, karate underwent a number of changes in practice and philosophy, making it more congruent with traditional Japanese martial arts. In keeping with these changes, it was thought that the original names of the forms might prove confusing, so they were Japanized at that time. In the present day also, the changes in terminology have sometimes been confusing to practitioners of different styles, who may refer to them by different names. Discussed below are many of the kata and their name changes, with some facts pertaining to their origin and practice.[1]

Shorin Kata

The most well-known kata of the Shorin school are the five Heian kata, called Pinan in Okinawa. The name Heian 平安 means "peace and tranquillity" and indicates that those proficient in these kata should feel at ease in any situation. Based on the kata Kanku Dai (see below), they were developed by Anko Itosu in the early 1900s and were introduced by him in 1905 into the physical education curriculum of the Okinawan school system. Itosu's intent was that they serve the dual purpose of physical education and self-defense.

The Bassai 抜塞 kata, Bassai Dai and Bassai Sho (Bassai "major" and "minor," respectively,) have maintained their original names, although in

Okinawa they are called Passai. Bassai means "to break through the enemy's defenses by shifting and finding the weak points." The original form, Bassai Dai, is said to have been developed by Matsumura Sokon and practiced primarily in Tomari or Shuri. Bassai Sho is a later, unique version of the *dai* form; it was created by Anko Itosu.

The kata Kanku Dai was formerly known as Kushanku (in Japanese, Koshokun), having taken its name from a Chinese martial artist who came to Okinawa in the eighteenth century. Kanku 観空 means "to observe the universe or sky," a name which gives meaning to the opening move, in which the performer views the sky through his upwardly raised hands. Kanku Dai is a very long form and has many variations. Anko Itosu developed a variation which became known as Kanku Sho. This kata is characterized by dynamic shifts and leaps.

Empi 燕飛, a light, speedy form that mimics the "flight of the swallow," is a rapid kata characterized by upward and downward movement and quick shifting. Its former name was Wansu, or Wanshu, after a Chinese military officer who was active in the martial arts on Okinawa. It was practiced only in the Tomari area until just after the time of the Meiji Restoration, when it began to spread to Shuri and Naha.

Gankaku 岩鶴, formerly known as Chinto, means "crane on a rock." This is an apt name, since the characteristic position of this form is an imitation of a crane poised on one leg about to strike out in defense. It is a very old form and has undergone changes over the years. One version, the one practiced in Shotokan karate, was developed by Anko Itosu.

One of the longer forms in practice today is known as Gojushiho 五十四歩, which means "fifty-four steps"; it also has *dai* and *sho* forms. The former name for them is Useshi. Of Chinese origin, they were practiced in China until the twentieth century. Anko Itosu developed his own version of these as well, which were later incorporated into the Shotokan system by Gichin Funakoshi.

The Unsu 雨手 kata, whose name means "hands like the clouds," implying that the hands sweep away the opponent's moves like clouds sweep across the sky, is a very old form. Its origin is unknown. Along with the Nijushiho form, it was borrowed from the Shito-ryu system of Kenwa Mabuni by Gichin Funakoshi and was incorporated into Shotokan karate.

Other Shorin forms in practice today include Wankan 王冠, or "king's crown"; Nijushiho 二十四歩, "twenty-four steps"; and Chinte 珍手, "unusual hands."

Shorei Kata

Tekki 鉄騎, which means "iron horse," is a series of three kata in which the movements are performed in the straddle, or horse-riding, stance. Originally known as Naihanchi, the forms are characterized by strong, deliberate movements to the side in a low stance. The origin of the first kata of the series is obscure, but it was practiced predominantly in Shuri. The second and third forms were added by Anko Itosu.

In present-day practice, the kata Hangetsu 半月, "half-moon," is noted for its strong performance, its half-moon steps, and crescent stance. It was formerly known as Seisan, or Seishan, and is of Chinese origin. It was practiced in Naha.

The Jion 慈恩 form has not undergone any name changes. According to legend, it was named after a Chinese monk who visited Okinawa. Originally, it was practiced primarily in Tomari.

Jutte 十手, or "ten hands," is another form that has not changed name. Originating in Tomari, its philosophy indicates that one should be able to perform the movements of ten men if faced with assailants. Sometimes the romanization of the characters is *jitte*.

The Sochin 壮鎮 form is characterized by low, powerful movements in the *sochin* stance. The name Sochin means "the preservation of peace among men." The Shotokan version was modified by Gikko Funakoshi, son of Gichin Funakoshi.

In all there estimated to be well over fifty kata that have been practiced throughout the history of Okinawan-Japanese karate, each having variations. The names of some of the other forms are Sanchin, Seiunchin, and Meikyo.

MODERN PRACTICE OF KATA

Most of the modern schools of the karate employ kata from both the Shorin and Shorei schools. In his book *Karate-do Kyohan* Master Funakoshi recommended the practice of fifteen kata for use in the Shotokan system.[2] From the Shorin school he selected the five Heian kata, as well as the Bassai, Kanku, Empi, and Gankaku kata. From the Shorei style he chose the three Tekki kata and the Jutte, Hangetsu, and Jion kata. It was his contention that knowledge of these fifteen would be sufficient if one were to practice them seriously. Although only fifteen were selected for basic practice, other kata practiced by Shotokan stylists include but are not limited to the Nijushiho, Sochin, Unsu,

Chinto, Gojushiho, Wankan, and Meikyo kata. Rather than emphasizing training in many different forms, however, it is of far more importance to train in one or two extensively.

The sequence in which kata are learned in the International Shotokan Karate Federation is shown in the following list. For promotion to the rank shown in the left-hand column, the form listed in the right-hand column must be performed successfully. Students begin by learning five Shorin Kata and then progress to a Shorei form. From that point on there is basically a free choice of kata, with it being generally acknowledged that a student should alternate between styles to balance out his technique. (Note that *shodan, nidan, sandan, yodan,* and *godan* simply mean first, second, third, fourth, and fifth level, respectively.)

Rank		*Kata*
8th *kyu*	—	Heian Shodan
7th *kyu*	—	Heian Nidan
6th *kyu*	—	Heian Sandan
5th *kyu*	—	Heian Yodan
4th *kyu*	—	Heian Godan
3rd *kyu*	—	Tekki Shodan
2nd *kyu*	—	Individual choice (see Appendix)
1st *kyu*	—	Individual choice (see Appendix)
Shodan (1st *dan*)	—	(see Appendix)

At Shodan (first-degree black-belt) level and above, two kata are performed in each promotion examination: one chosen by the examiner and one by the performer. The kata to be chosen from are shown in the Appendix.

SELECTED KATA

On the following pages are presented nine representative kata of the Shotokan system, chosen to exhibit a balance between Shorin and Shorei forms. Further, mastery of the Heian series and the kata Bassai Dai and Tekki Shodan will allow the performer to take the first-degree black-belt exam. Also included are the Nijushiho and Sochin kata, practiced by more advanced students, usually of the third-degree level and above. They are not among the basic fifteen taught by Master Funakoshi as part of his system, but were selected because they are the author's favorite forms.

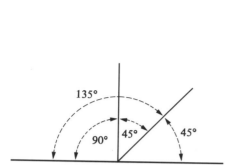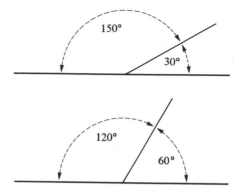

Accompanying the instructions for each kata is a diagram showing the *embusen,* or demonstration line, for that kata. (See sample on facing page.) The beginning and ending position of the kata is marked by a circle, and the numbered lines represent successive lead-foot positions. The small picture of a camera shows the angle from which the photographs for all the kata were taken.

The photographs which accompany the instructions show the moves of the kata. The numbered photographs show when the lead foot *first* lands in the corresponding numbered position of the *embusen.* The unnumbered photographs show moves done while in these positions and also intermediate positions. The numbers in parentheses in the kata instructions correspond to those of the *embusen* and photographs.

With the above in mind, there are several important points to remember in following the instructions for the kata. Note that all kata begin and end at the same point. At this point, the body is in the *yoi,* or ready, position. The final position is also known as *zanshin* (lit., perfect finish), which indicates that the performer is still ready to face opponents. After pausing for a few moments in this position, the performer may relax.

In taking successive steps in the long, straight portions of the *embusen,* the feet are naturally shoulder width apart. They therefore do not literally step onto the numbered points, but land to the left and the right of the line. (See positions 6–8 and 14–16 of the sample *embusen.*) The *embusen* diagrams should be thought of as guidelines for position.

It should be understood that angle measurements other than 90, 180, and 270 degrees are not intended to be precise, but serve as approximations for direction. The diagrams given here may serve as a guide to performing the kata correctly. A pivot of 180 degrees simply means a pivot to the rear; a pivot of 270 degrees means a $\frac{3}{4}$-turn. The instructions should be followed in conjunction with the *embusen.*

Finally, remember that you are fighting as you are performing the kata. In a fight you must see the attacker before you can defend against him. So before you turn to meet a new attacker, make sure that you look in the direction from which the attack is coming.

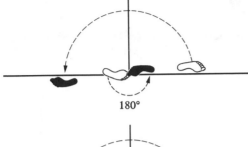

Pivot on the right foot 180 degrees to the left (at the same time the left foot swings 180 degrees to the left).

180°

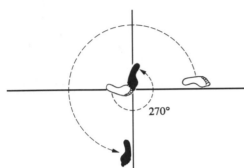

Pivot on the right foot 270 degrees to the left (at the same time the left foot swings 270 degrees to the left).

270°

Note: The white feet show the starting position; the black feet show the final position.

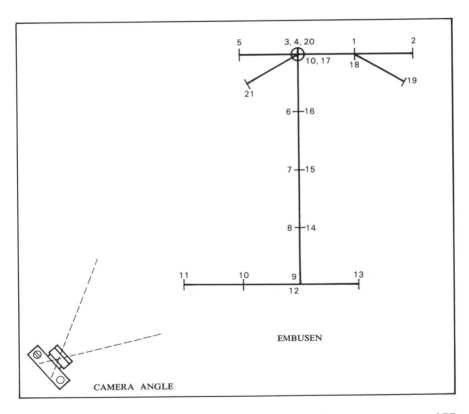

Ready position ⟶ **1**

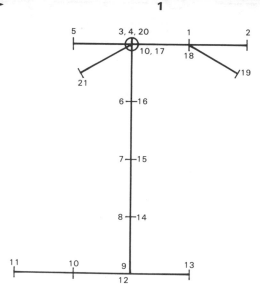

■ Heian Shodan

Note: All unspecified stances for this kata are the front stance.

Begin in the ready position, facing down the center line of the *embusen*. Look to the left and step out with the left foot to the front stance, performing a left downward block (Fig. 1). Step forward and execute a right lunge punch to the midsection (2). Look over the right shoulder and bring the right foot back in a sweeping motion as you pivot 180 degrees to the right, landing in the right front stance and performing a right downward block (3). Draw the right foot back halfway and bring the right hammer fist in a circular motion to the left temple. Then, simultaneously slide the right foot back to its original position and execute a right bottom-fist strike (4). Step forward, executing a left lunge punch to the midsection (5).

Slide the left foot 90 degrees to the left, keeping the left front stance and performing a left downward block (6). Perform a left rising knife-hand block;

156 · PART TWO: KARATE TRAINING

2

3

4

5

6

7   8   9   →

follow this immediately by stepping forward and performing a right rising block (7). Step forward and perform a left rising block (8). Step forward with a right rising block; *kiai* (9).

Bring the left foot to the right in a sweeping motion, pivoting on the right foot 270 degrees to the left, ending up in the left front stance. As you are turning, perform a left downward block (10). Step forward and perform a right lunge punch (11). Pivot on the left foot 180 degrees to the right, performing a right downward block as you assume the right front stance (12). Step forward and execute a left lunge punch to the midsection (13).

Pivot on the right foot 90 degrees to the left and perform a left downward block as you assume the left front stance (14). Step forward and execute a right lunge punch to the midsection (15). Step forward and perform a left lunge punch to the midsection (16). Again, step forward and make a right lunge punch to the midsection; *kiai* (17).

Bring the left foot up to the right as you pivot on the right foot 270 degrees to the left into the left back stance. As you are turning, perform a left knife-hand block (18). Step out 30 degrees to the right with the right foot and execute a right knife-hand block in the right back stance (19). Pivot on the left foot 150 degrees to the right, ending up in the right back stance and executing a right knife-hand block (20). Step out 30 degrees to the left with the left foot and execute a left knife-hand block in the left back stance (21). Keeping the right foot in place, pivot 60 degrees to the left, stepping to the *zanshin* position.

10   11   →

12   13   →

14   15   16   17

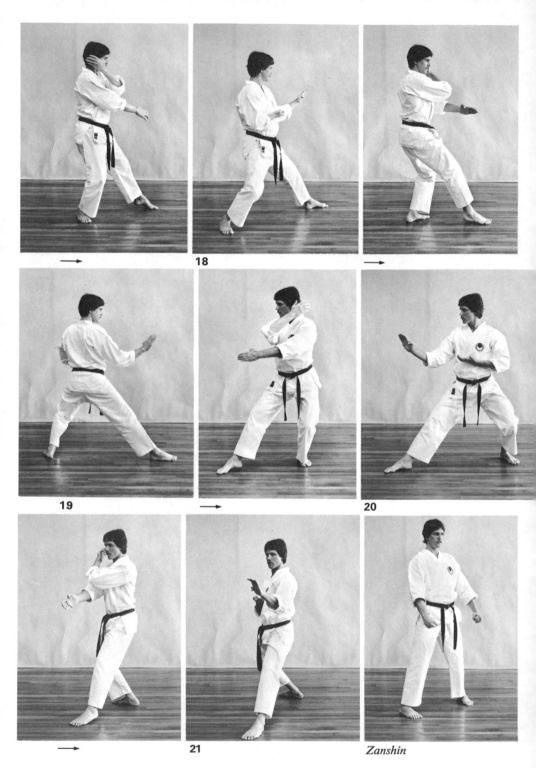

18

19

20

→

21

Zanshin

Ready position   →   **1**

■ Heian Nidan

Begin in the ready position, facing down the center line of the *embusen*. Look to the left and step out with the left foot to the back stance, simultaneously performing a left backhand block and a right rising block (Fig. 1). While in place, simultaneously execute a right close punch and a left outside forearm-block. Perform a left bottom-fist strike as you withdraw the right hand

→ **2** →

to the side. Look to the right and shift into the right back stance in place, bringing the fists to the left side (2). In position, simultaneously execute a right backhand block and a left rising block. Then, simultaneously perform a left close punch and a right outside forearm-block. Perform a right bottom-fist strike while withdrawing the left hand. Bring the hands to the left side, right fist above left, as you bring the left foot halfway to the right foot (3).

Bring the right foot up to the left knee as you make a half turn to the right. Execute a right side snap-kick and a right back-fist strike simultaneously. Withdraw the kicking foot to the left knee, and bring the hands to the preparatory position for the knife-hand block. Step back with the right foot to the back stance and execute a left knife-hand block (4). Step forward (back stance) and execute a right knife-hand block (5). Step forward (back stance) and execute a left knife-hand block (6). Step forward to the right front stance. As you move to this position, make a sweeping block with your left hand and execute a right spear-hand thrust to the solar plexus. The finished position has the back of the left hand placed under the elbow of the right arm. *Kiai* as you perform this move (7).

3

4 5 6 7

8

9

Pivot 270 degrees to the left on the right foot, stepping into the left back stance and performing a knife-hand block with the left hand (8). Step out 30 degrees to the right and execute a right knife-hand block in the right back stance (9). Pivot 150 degrees to the right on the left foot, ending up in the right back stance and executing a right knife-hand block (10). Step out 30 degrees to the left and perform a left knife-hand block in the left back stance (11). Keeping the right foot in place, pivot 60 degrees to the left into the left front stance and execute a right inside forearm-block (12).

Perform a right front kick, stepping down in the front stance. Counter-punch with the left fist to the midsection (13). Then, simultaneously shift the right foot back a few inches and perform a left inside forearm-block. The hips should twist to the right and the left shoulder should be slightly forward.

10

11

12

13

14

15

Perform a left front kick and land in the left front stance. Perform a right counterpunch to the midsection (14). Step forward with the right foot into the front stance and perform a right augmented forearm-block (15). In this position the body is half-facing (twisted inward about 45 degrees) and the left fist rests against the right elbow.

Pivot 270 degrees to the left on the right foot, performing a left downward block in the left front stance (16). Look 30 degrees to the right and perform a left rising block with the knife hand. Step out 30 degrees to the right to the right front stance and perform a right rising block with the closed fist (17). Pivot 150 degrees to the right on the left foot and perform a right downward block in the front stance (18). Look 30 degrees to the left and perform a rising block with the right knife hand. Step out 30 degrees to the left to the left front stance and perform a left rising block with the closed fist; *kiai* as you do this move (19). Keeping the right foot in place, pivot 60 degrees to the left, stepping to the *zanshin* position.

166 · PART TWO: KARATE TRAINING

16

17

18

19

Zanshin

Ready position →

```
    3, 4, 13
 ├────⊕─┤
15      14, 15  1, 2, 14

    5─┼12

    6─┼11

    7─┼10

    8─┴9
```

■ **Heian Sandan**

Note: In this kata, positions 14 and 15 are the straddle stance. In the *embusen* there are two 14s and two 15s, showing the placement of both feet in each position.

Begin in the ready position, facing down the center line of the *embusen*. Look to the left and then step out to the left in the back stance while executing a left inside forearm-block (Fig. 1). Bring the right foot up to the left foot; as you do so, simultaneously perform a right inside forearm-block and a left downward block (2). Standing in place, perform a left inside forearm-block and a right downward block. Look to the rear right and pivot 180 degrees to the right on the left foot, ending up in the right back stance and performing a right inside forearm-block (3). Bring the left foot up to the right foot as you execute a left inside forearm-block and a right downward block (4). Standing in place, execute a right inside forearm-block and a left downward block simultaneously.

1

2

3

4

5

6

→ 7

Look to the left and step out 90 degrees to the left back stance as you perform a left augmented forearm-block(5). Step forward to the right front stance and execute a right spear-hand thrust to the midsection (6). In this position, the left hand rests under the right elbow, palm down. Pivot on the right foot to the left as shown. Completing the turn, bring the left foot forward into the straddle stance and perform a left bottom-fist strike (7). Step forward to the right front stance and execute a right lunge punch; *kiai* as you do this move (8).

Slowly bring the left foot to the right foot as you pivot on the right foot 180 degrees to the left. Bring the hands to the position shown (9). Bring the right knee up high and stomp down on your opponent's foot, ending up in the straddle stance. As your foot comes down, the right arm performs the block shown (here called the "bent-arm" block) (10). Execute a right back-fist strike to the face. Return the right hand to blocking position, and bring the left leg up and stomp down into the straddle stance. As your foot comes down, perform a left "bent-arm" block (11). Execute a left back-fist strike to the face

170 · PART TWO: KARATE TRAINING

8   9

10

11

12

and return the fist to the blocking position. Bring the right foot up and stomp down into the straddle stance, performing a right "bent-arm" block (12). Execute a right back-fist strike and return the fist to the blocking position. Extend the right hand in a vertical knife-hand block as you step forward to the left front stance and perform a left lunge punch (13).

Bring the right foot up to the left foot and then out to the right in the straddle stance. Pivot on the right foot 180 degrees to the left into the straddle stance, performing a right forefist punch over your left shoulder and a left elbow strike to the rear (14). Shift about 18 inches (45 cm.) to your right and perform a left forefist punch over the right shoulder and a right elbow strike to the rear; *kiai* as you do this move (15). Return to the *zanshin* position by bringing both feet to the point of origin.

13

14   15   *Zanshin*

Ready position ⟶ **1**

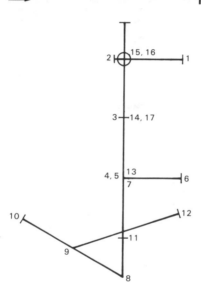

■ Heian Yodan

Begin in the ready position, facing down the main line of the *embusen*. Look to the left and slowly step out to the left back stance, slowly bringing the knife hands up to the blocking position shown (Fig. 1). Slowly bringing the hands down, look to the right and twist the hips and legs to the right back stance (2). Bring the hands up to the blocking position shown. Slide the left foot halfway to the right and then step out to the left front stance, performing a downward cross-block, right fist over left (3). Step forward to the right back stance and perform a right augmented forearm-block (4). Move the left foot up to the right knee, look 90 degrees to the left, and place the left fist on top of the right (5). Then, simultaneously execute a left side snap-kick and a left back-fist strike to the left.

Step into the left front stance and perform a right elbow strike (6). Look

2

3

4

5

6

7

to the rear (right) as you shift your left foot to the center line of your body. Then, simultaneously bring your right hand to your left side and your right foot up to your left knee. Perform a right side snap-kick and a right back-fist strike. Step into the right front stance and strike your right hand with a left elbow strike (7). Look 90 degrees to the left and perform a left downward sweeping-block and a right rising block. Snap the hips to the left, shifting into the left front stance, and execute a right knife-hand strike and a left rising block with the open hand. Perform a right front snap-kick to the face; then step to the position shown and perform a right back-fist strike; *kiai* (8).

Pivot 240 degrees to the left right foot into the left back stance. Quickly bring the fists up in front of the face, wrists crossed and palms inward, right arm toward you (9). Slowly bring the hands down and turn the fists as you perform a wedge block. Stepping forward, perform a right front snap-kick to the face. As your right foot comes down in the front stance, perform a right lunge punch to the midsection (10). Follow with a left counterpunch to the midsection.

8

9

10

11

12

Slowly pivot on the left foot about 135 degrees to the right and perform a wedge block, right arm toward you, in the right back stance (11). Perform a front snap-kick with the left foot. As your left foot comes down in the front stance, perform a left lunge punch to the midsection (12). Follow with a right counterpunch to the midsection. Look to the left, moving the fists as shown, and slide the left foot to the left, back to the main line of the *embusen* (about 75 degrees), and execute a left augmented forearm-block in the left back stance (13). Step forward to the right back stance and perform a right augmented forearm-block (14). Step forward again, to the left back stance, and perform a left augmented forearm-block (15). Twist the hips forward into the front stance and thrust both knife hands forward to grab the opponent's neck. Pull the opponent's neck down as you execute a right knee kick; *kiai* as you do this move.

Pivot 180 degrees to the left on the left (lead) foot, performing a left knife-hand block as you come into the left back stance (16). Step forward to the right back stance and execute a right knife-hand block (17). Keep the foot in place and step back to the *zanshin* position.

13

14

15

16

17

Zanshin

Ready position **1** →

```
                    3, 4
        12, 14 ──⊕──┤1, 2

   8, 11, 13, 15 ─┤5

                 ─┤6

                 ─┤7
                 9, 10
```

■ Heian Godan

Begin in the ready position, facing down the long line of the *embusen*. Look left and step out to the left back stance, executing a left inside forearm-block (Fig. 1). Follow with a right reverse punch to the midsection. Slowly draw the right foot to the left foot and assume the position shown (2). Step to the right back stance and execute a right inside forearm-block (3). Perform a left reverse punch to the midsection. Draw the left foot slowly to the right foot and bring the hands to the position shown (4).

Step forward into the right back stance and execute a right augmented forearm-block (5). Step forward to the left front stance and perform a downward cross-block, right wrist over left (6). Then perform a high cross-block with the knife hands, right wrist over left. Bring the hands to the position shown and strike out with a left bottom-fist strike. Step to the right front stance and perform a right lunge punch to the midsection; *kiai* (7).

180 · PART TWO: KARATE TRAINING

2

3

→

4

5

6

→

→

→

7

8

9

Pivot on the left foot 180 degrees to the left; land by stomping down on your opponent's leg in the straddle stance and executing a right downward block (8). Slowly extend the left back hand to the left side. Execute a right crescent kick, landing in the straddle stance, and follow with a right elbow strike to your left palm (9). Cross the left foot behind the right and execute a right augmented forearm-block (10). Look left and step out slightly with the left foot. Jab upward with the right hand.

Jump in the air, turning 90 degrees to the left, and land in the position shown, executing a downward cross-block, right wrist over left; *kiai* as you jump (11). Step to the right front stance and execute a right augmented forearm-block (12).

Turn the hips to face the opposite direction and bring the hands to the position shown. Lower yourself to the left front stance and simultaneously perform a right knife-hand strike to groin and a left sweeping block (13). In place, shift into the back stance, and simultaneously perform a downward

10

11

12

13

14

15

Zanshin

block with the left hand a high inside-block with the right hand. Slowly bring the left foot back to the right foot (14). Rotate your feet 90 degrees to the left and bring the hands to the position shown. Step to the right front stance, simultaneously performing a left knife-hand strike to the groin and a right sweeping block (15). In place, shift into the back stance; simultaneously perform a right downward block and a left high inside forearm-block. Bring the right foot back to the *zanshin* position.

Ready position   →   →

1   →

1, 3 ⊕ 2

■ **Tekki Shodan**

Begin in the ready position. Bring the feet and hands together, placing the left palm over the right hand. Step across with the right foot and stomp kick down into the straddle stance while performing a right backhand block (Fig. 1). Strike the right palm with a left elbow strike. Looking to the left, bring the

fists to the right side, left fist over right. Execute a left downward block and then a right hook punch.

Step across in front and perform a left stomping kick. As your foot comes down into the straddle stance, execute a right inside forearm-block (2). (The next move shown is the intermediate position of the arms as they perform the next block.) Execute a right downward block and a left guiding block simultaneously. Execute a left back-fist strike with the right fist under the left elbow. Look left and perform an inside sweeping-block with the left leg, and then a left augmented forearm-block.

Look right and perform an inside sweeping-block with the right leg, and then a left augmented forearm-block to the right. Looking to the left, bring the fists to the right side, left fist over right. Perform a left bottom-fist strike

186 • PART TWO: KARATE TRAINING

and a right hook punch simultaneously; *kiai* as you do this move. Slowly extend the left hand in a backhand block. Strike the left palm with a right elbow strike. Looking to the right, bring the fists to the left side, right fist over left, and perform a right downward block and then a left hook punch.

Step across in the front and perform a right stomping kick. As your foot comes down into the straddle stance, execute a left inside forearm-block (3). Execute a left downward block and a right guiding block simultaneously. Perform a right back-fist strike, with the left fist under the right elbow. Look right and perform an inside sweeping-block with the right leg.

Perform a right augmented forearm-block to the right. Perform an inside

3

Zanshin

sweeping-block with the left leg and then a right augmented forearm-block to the left. Looking to the right, bring the fists to the left side, right fist over left. Simultaneously strike to the right side with a right bottom-fist strike and a left hook punch; *kiai* as you do this move. Slowly withdraw the right foot to the left foot. In this position, the open left hand is over the right. Assume the *zanshin* position.

Ready position

■ **Bassai Dai**

Begin in the ready position, facing down the long line of the *embusen*. Bring the feet together by sliding both of them in, and grasp the right fist with the left hand. Take a sliding step forward with the right foot; bring the left foot behind the right as shown and perform a right augmented forearm-block. The fingertips of left hand are pressed against the right wrist (Fig. 1). Pivot to

the rear on the right foot, ending up in the left front stance and executing a
left inside forearm-block (2). Execute a right inside forearm-block. Shift to
the rear in place, to the right front stance, and execute a left outside-forearm
block (3). Then perform a right inside forearm-block.

Bring the right foot back to the left foot and turn 90 degrees to the right.
Step forward into the right front stance, performing a right scooping block
from inside to outside and then a right outside forearm-block (4). Perform a
left inside forearm-block. Twist 90 degrees to the left, withdrawing the left
foot slightly and bringing the hands to the right side, left fist over right (5).
Slowly extend the left hand in a vertical knife-hand block. Perform a right
straight punch to the midsection. Then, twist to the left into the left front
stance, performing a right inside forearm-block to the right side. Return from
the front stance to the immediately previous position as you perform a left
straight punch to the midsection. Then, twist to the right into the right front
stance. Perform a left inside forearm-block to the left.

6   7   8

9

Pivoting on the left foot 90 degrees to the left, step to the right back stance and execute a right knife-hand block (6). Step forward twice (back stances), performing first a left and then a right knife-hand block (7, 8). Step back to the left back stance and execute a left knife-hand block (9). Twist the rear foot inward slightly as you move the hands in a clockwise circular movement and grasp the opponent's arm. The fingertips of the open left hand are placed on the right forearm at the end of this move. Pull the opponent in as you perform a right side thrust-kick to his knee; *kiai*. Withdraw the kicking foot and then step back with it, ending up in the left back stance and performing a left knife-hand block (10). Step forward (back stance) and execute a right knife-hand block (11). Withdraw the right foot to the left foot and bring the fists to the chest (12). Slowly raise them to the position shown to break the opponent's hold.

10

11   12

13   14   15

16   →   17

Step forward into the right front stance, striking with both bottom fists to the opponent's sides (13). Take a sliding step forward and execute a right lunge punch to the midsection (14). Twist to the rear in place, ending up in the left front stance, and strike to the opponent's groin with a right knife-hand strike while blocking with the left knife hand (15). Slowly withdraw the left foot to the right foot and perform a left downward block and a high right inside forearm-block (16).

Pivot on the left foot 180 degrees to the left and stomp down with the right foot, landing in the straddle stance and performing a right downward block (17). Extend a left backhand block to the left, and then perform a right crescent kick, using the left hand as a target. Land in the straddle stance and perform a right elbow strike using the left palm as a target (18). Alternately execute a right, left, and right augmented downward-block. Shift 90 degrees to the right by moving your right foot over, and assume the right front stance, while bringing the hands to the left side, the right fist over the left (19). Perform a double punch *(yama-tsuki),* left hand on top. Withdraw the right

(second view)   **20**   **21**

22   **23**   **24**

foot to the left foot and bring the hands to the right side, the left fist over the right (20). Step forward to the left front stance and execute a double punch, right hand on top (21). Withdraw the left foot and bring the hands to the left side, the right fist over the left (22). Step forward to the right front stance and perform a double punch, left hand on top (23).

Pivot on the right foot 270 degrees to the left, ending up in a low left front stance and performing a right scooping block (24). Twist the feet to the right front stance and perform a left scooping block (25). Slide the left foot up to the right foot, step out 45 degrees to the left into the right back stance, and perform a right knife-hand block (26). Slowly and with increasing tension, turn on the left foot 90 degrees to the right, maintaining the right back stance, and perform a right knife-hand block (27). Slide the right foot halfway up to the left foot and then step forward to the left back stance, performing a left knife-hand block; *kiai* (28). Withdraw the left foot to the right foot and grasp the right fist with the left hand. Move the left foot out to the *zanshin* position.

25

→

26

27

→

28

→

Zanshin

Ready position   →   **1**

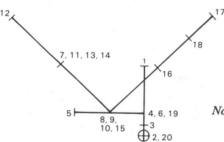

Note: 1 shows the position of the rear foot.

■ Nijushiho

Begin in the ready position. Slide step back into the left back stance and execute a sweeping block with the left hand, as shown (Fig. 1). Shift forward, sharply performing a right counterpunch to the midsection. Slowly slide step forward to the position shown and bring the left forearm up under your opponent's elbow as you pull his hand toward you with your right hand (2). Pivot 180 degrees to the right on the left foot, crossing the hands in front of the face and then bringing them to the sides. Assume the right hourglass stance and perform a double punch, right hand on top (3). Raise the right knee sharply and bring the fists together with the palms toward the face. Cross the right fist over the left and bring the right foot down in the front stance, executing a wedge block (4). Look left and step out 90 degrees with the left foot to the front stance (5). Execute a left rising block with the knife hand and then a right rising elbow-strike.

6

Twist your body to the rear (to the right), ending up in the straddle stance; extend your right hand in a vertical knife-hand block (6). Pull the opponent in with your right hand as you perform a right side thrust-kick and then a left hook punch. Facing left, slowly extend the left hand in a vertical knife-hand block. Pull the opponent in with your left hand and perform a left side thrust-kick and then a right hook punch. Shift the left foot back to a position slightly behind the right foot, as shown, and step out 45 degrees with the right foot to the front stance, executing simultaneously a left palm-heel strike to the face and a right palm-heel strike to the midsection (7).

Twist your body to the rear (to the left) into the left front stance and execute a right ridge-hand strike to the neck and a low left palm-heel block (8). Bring the right foot up to the left foot and strike the right palm with the back of the left hand in the raised position; *kiai* (9). Step back with the left foot to the right front stance and perform a right pressing block (10). The left hand is held palm up under the right elbow. Execute a double punch downward, left hand on top. Slowly twist your body to the rear (to the left) into the left back

11 **12**

13 **14**

stance and extend a left backhand block (11). Step forward into the straddle
stance and execute a right rising elbow-strike (12). Perform a left straight
punch to the midsection. Slide both feet to the left as you perform a right
downward block (13). In place, twist the feet into the left back stance and
extend a left backhand block (14). Step forward into the straddle stance and
strike the left palm with a right elbow strike (15). Then perform a right augmented downward-block. (The elbow strike and augmented downward-
block are shown in front and rear views.)

Step forward with the left foot into the back stance and extend a left backhand block (16). Step forward in the straddle stance and execute a right rising
elbow-strike and then a left straight punch to the midsection (17). Then,
shift back about one foot (30 cm.) as you execute a right downward block

15

(second view)

(second view)

16

17

18

19

20   →   →   *Zanshin*

(18). Pivot 135 degrees to the left on the left foot and step to the right into the left hourglass stance (19). Cross both hands in front of the face, bring them to the sides, and execute a double punch, right hand on top; *kiai* as you do this. Perform a circular block, stepping forward to the right hourglass stance. As your lead (right) foot stops, execute a double palm-heel strike *(kiai)* left hand on top (20). Bring the right foot back to the *zanshin* position.

Ready position

→

1

■ **Sochin**

Note: In the photos for this kata there is no 17 shown, since the foot is in this position for only an instant.

Begin in the ready position. Slowly step forward with the right foot and assume the *sochin* stance, performing a right downward block and a left rising block (Fig. 1). This move is done slowly and with increasing tension. Slowly

2

3   4   5

step forward into the left *sochin* stance, extending a right vertical knife-hand block (2). Perform a left and then a right straight punch to the midsection. Pivot on the right foot 90 degrees to the left into the left back stance, performing a left downward block and a high right inside forearm-block (3). This move is done sharply. Quickly step forward into the right *sochin* stance, performing a left rising block and a right downward block (4). Slowly step forward into the left *sochin* stance, extending a right vertical knife-hand block (5). Perform a left and then a right straight punch to the midsection.

Pivot sharply on the right foot 180 degrees to the left and assume the left back stance, performing a left downward block and a high right inside forearm-block (6). Quickly step forward to the right *sochin* stance, performing a left rising block and a right downward block (7). Slowly step forward into the left *sochin* stance, extending a right vertical knife-hand block (8). Perform a left and then a right straight punch to the midsection.

Pivot on the right foot 90 degrees to the left, drawing the left foot up to the right knee. Perform a left side snap-kick and a left back-fist strike simultane-

9

10

11

12

ously. Come down in the left *sochin* stance (facing 180 degrees from position 8) and perform a right elbow strike using the left palm as target (9). Bring the right foot to the left knee and pivot on the left foot 90 degrees to the right. Perform a right side snap-kick and a right back-fist strike simultaneously. Come down in the right *sochin* stance (facing 180 degrees from position 9) and perform a left elbow strike using the palm as a target (10). Keeping the left foot in place, pivot 180 degrees to the right and perform a right knife-hand block in the right back stance (11). Step out 45 degrees to the left into the left back stance and perform a left knife-hand block (12). Pivot 135 de-

13   **14**   **15**

16   ⟶   (second view)

grees to the left on the right foot and execute a left knife-hand block in the left back stance (13).

Step out 30 degrees to the right into the right back stance, performing a right knife-hand block (14). Pivot 60 degrees to the right on the left foot, in the right back stance, performing a right knife-hand block (15). Step forward to the left back stance, performing a left knife-hand block (16). Slide the right foot forward and thrust a right close-range spear hand, palm up, to the opponent's stomach. The left hand is placed under the right elbow, palm

18   (second view)

down. Follow with a left front kick. As soon as your left foot lands from this kick (position 17), immediately perform a right front kick, striking forward with the left back fist and performing a right guiding block while the right foot is still in the air. As you come down in the right *sochin* stance, perform a back-fist strike with the right fist and a guiding block with the left fist; *kiai* (18). Pivot 180 degrees to the left on the left foot and strike the left palm with a right crescent kick. Land in the right *sochin* stance, performing a left rising block and a right downward block (19).

Step out 45 degrees to the left, performing a left inside forearm-block in the left *sochin* stance (20). Step forward, executing a right lunge punch in the right *sochin* stance (21). Pivot 90 degrees to the right on the left foot, still in the right *sochin* stance, performing a right inside forearm-block (22). Then step forward in the left *sochin* stance, executing a left lunge punch (23).

Shift the left foot over 45 degrees to the left, still in the left *sochin* stance, performing a left inside forearm-block (24). Follow with a right inside fore-

19

20

21

22

23

24

Zanshin

arm-block. Perform a right front kick in place, and return to the left *sochin* stance, slowly and with tension performing a left straight punch to the midsection and pulling the opponent in with the right hand. Perform a right and then a left straight punch to the midsection. On the second punch, *kiai*. Step back to the *zanshin* position.

Appendix: Karate Ranks

The requirements for the attainment of successive ranks currently granted by the International Shotokan Karate Federation, a branch of the Japan Karate Association (JKA), are shown in Tables 5 and 6 (pp. 216, 217). The Basics, Kumite, and Kata which must be performed successfully in order to achieve the rank listed in the first column of the respective line are outlined. It should be noted that the examiner may vary the basic techniques and type of kumite required at each level if he so desires.

Table 5 shows the requirements for the *kyu*-level ranks, in which one proceeds from 8th *kyu* to 1st *kyu*. Table 6 shows the requirement for the *dan* level, in which one moves from 1st *kyu* to Shodan (1st *dan*) and then up through Godan (5th *dan*) and beyond (see Table 8, p. 218). *Dan* examinees must perform two kata, noted in the fourth column of Table 6 and in the separate Kata-Selection Chart. One kata is selected by the examinee himself, and the other by the examiner. The kata which the examinee chooses may be repeated in successive examinations, if desired.

WHAT JUDGES LOOK FOR

For basic techniques (see Tables 5 and 6) there are certain points which the examining judges pay particular attention to. Most important are correct form, attitude, understanding of technique, balance, movement, and spirit. As the student becomes more advanced, increasing ability in speed and focus consistent with rank is expected. Colored belts (see Table 7) should demonstrate increased ability in all the areas above, with marked improvement in body shifting and counterattacking.

Basic elements to be aware of in performing the kumite are distancing, timing, form and technique, body-shifting ability, and correct adaptation to different opponents.

In judging kata, the examiners observe deportment, position of body, posture, stance, basic techniques, correct application of power, speed of technique, body expansion and contraction, line of movement, body movement,

Table 5
REQUIREMENTS FOR THE KYU-LEVEL RANKS

Rank	Basics	Kumite	Kata
8th *kyu*	Lunge punch; rising block; forearm block; downward block; knife-hand block; front kick; front stance; back stance	3-attack sparring	Heian Shodan
7th *kyu*	(As above)	3-attack sparring	Heian Nidan
6th *kyu*	Add to above: blocking a counterpunch; side thrust- and side snap-kicks; straddle stance	1- or 3-attack sparring (examiner's choice)	Heian Sandan
5th *kyu*	Add: triple punch; counter-punches with all blocks; front kicks in succession	1-attack sparring	Heian Yodan
4th *kyu*	(As above)	1-attack sparring	Heian Godan
3rd *kyu*	Add roundhouse kick	1-attack sparring	Tekki Shodan
2nd *kyu*	Add roundhouse kick with counterpunch	1-attack sparring using kicks and punches	Examinee's choice of one, usually from Bassai Dai, Kanku Dai, Hangetsu, Empi, Tekki Nidan*
1st *kyu*	Add front, side, and roundhouse kicks in succession	(As above)	(As above)

*The current practice in JKA clubs is to perform Bassai Dai.

interpretation, and continuity.[1] Naturally, as has already been mentioned, these factors are considered in accordance with the grade level. Examiners do not expect a white belt to adapt to his opponent in the same manner as a 3rd *dan* examinee.

BELT SYSTEM

The belts granted upon promotion to successive ranks are shown in Table 7. This system is fairly standard among karate organizations, at least as far as the point at which brown and black belts are awarded is concerned. Some variations are noted in the Table.

Table 6
REQUIREMENTS FOR THE DAN-LEVEL RANKS

Rank	Basics	Kumite	Kata
			(Examinee's selection/ Examiner's selection. Refer to Kata-Selection Chart.)
Shodan (1st *dan*)	Various combinations of blocks, punches, stances, and kicks, as required by examiner	Semi-free sparring	One from A/Any Heian or Tekki Shodan
Nidan (2nd *dan*)	Fewer combinations, but more complex ones	Free sparring	One from A or B/ One from A
Sandan (3rd *dan*)	Ability to instruct	Free sparring or self-defense techniques (examiner's choice)	One from A, B, or C/ One from A or B
Yodan (4th *dan*)	Demonstration of special research into fighting	(As above)	One from A, B, C, or D/ One from A, B, or C
Godan (5th *dan*)	Demonstration of further special research into fighting		One from A, B, C, or D/ One from A, B, or C

KATA-SELECTION CHART

A	B	C	D
Tekki Nidan	Tekki Sandan	Bassai Sho	Gojushiho Sho
Bassai Dai	Jion	Kanku Sho	Gojushiho Dai
Kanku Dai	Gankaku	Sochin	Unsu
Hangetsu	Jutte	Chinte	
Empi		Nijushiho	

Table 7
KARATE BELT-SYSTEM

Rank	Belt	
Kyu 8th 7th	White	*Note:* The informal term "colored belt" refers to 6th to 1st *kyu*. In JKA groups, a black belt is worn at all *dan* levels. In some other groups, however, holders of 6th, 7th, and 8th *dan* wear a red and white belt, and those of 9th and 10th *dan* a solid red belt. Other variations include a red stripe in the center of a black belt.
6th 5th 4th	Various colors according to organization; some continue with white	
3rd 2nd 1st	Brown	
Dan	Black	

Table 8
AGE AND OTHER REQUIREMENTS FOR
DAN-LEVEL RANKS AND SPECIAL TITLES

Rank	Minimum Age for Rank	Minimum Time in Training	Title	Requirements for Title
Shodan (1st *dan*)	(No minimum age until Rokudan)	3 years	—	—
Nidan (2nd *dan*)	—	1 year after Shodan	—	—
Sandan (3rd *dan*)	—	2 years after Nidan	—	—
Yodan (4th *dan*)	—	3 years after Sandan	—	—
Godan (5th *dan*)	—	3 years after Yodan	Renshi	At least 2 years after Godan; minimum age 35
Rokudan (6th *dan*)	35	5 years after Godan	(Renshi)	(As above)
Shichidan (7th *dan*)	42	7 years after Rokudan	Kyoshi	At least 10 years after Renshi
Hachidan (8th *dan*)	50	8 years after Shichidan	(Kyoshi)	(As above)
Kudan (9th *dan*)	60	10 years after Hachidan	Hanshi	At least 15 years after Kyoshi
Judan (10th *dan*)	70	10 years after Kudan	(Hanshi)	(As above)

NOTE ON THE HIGHER RANKS

In recent years there has been much confusion over the high ranks held by many young Americans. Numerous individuals in their early twenties and thirties have appeared billing themselves as "grand masters" with ranks from 6th to 10th *dan*. This phenomenon is unique to the Western world, as the Japanese are more cognizant of the requirements of rank; such preposterous claims would be ridiculed in Japan.

The minimum age requirements listed in Table 8 were set by the Federation of All-Japan Karate-Do Organizations in 1971. This organization consists of all major karate systems and organizations in Japan, and the grading that each uses follows these criteria.

The criteria for the bestowing of titles of Renshi, Kyoshi, and Hanshi shown in Table 8 were also set by the Federation in 1971. It should be noted that these titles are awarded for great achievement and are not automatically bestowed. A cursory examination of the Table will reveal that the achievers of the high ranks are all thirty-five years of age or older, with the top ranks reserved for masters sixty or older. Claims by Americans to high rank should be considered in light of current practice in Japan.

NOTE ON JUNIOR RANKS

According to current practices of the Japan Karate Association, ranks held by young people under the age of sixteen are considered junior grades, and such individuals may not be promoted beyond 3rd *dan*. Although the same test is administered to young people as to adults, age and development are taken into consideration during the examinations. Upon reaching the age of sixteen, black-belt holders of the 2nd and 3rd *dan* automatically revert to the lst *dan* and are then considered to be senior-grade holders of this degree. They may at that time take a reexamination for 2nd or 3rd *dan* if their progress and experience warrant it.

Notes

CHAPTER 1

1. E. Norman Gardiner, *Athletics of the Ancient World* (London: Oxford University Press, 1967), pp. 9–14.

2. Robert Flaceliere, *Daily Life in Greece* (New York: Macmillan Co., 1965), p. 107.

3. Marjorie Quennel and C. H. B. Quennel, *Everyday Things in Ancient Greece,* rev. ed., ed. Kathleen Freeman (New York: G. P. Putnam's Sons, 1968), p. 160.

4. Plato, *The Laws,* trans. A. E. Taylor (New York: E. P. Dutton, 1960), pp. 200–201.

5. Gardiner, *Athletics of the Ancient World,* p. 15.

6. Masatatsu Oyama, *Waga Karate Gorin no Sho* (Tokyo: Kodansha, 1955), p. 92.

7. For a comprehensive list, see Donn F. Draeger and Robert W. Smith, *Comprehensive Asian Fighting Arts* (Tokyo: Kodansha International, 1969), pp. 199–202.

8. Bruce A. Haines, *Karate's History and Traditions* (Rutland and Tokyo: Charles E. Tuttle Co., 1968), p. 72.

9. Earl R. Bull, *Ryuku: The Floating Dragon* (Newark, Ohio: Earl R. Bull, 1958), p. 186.

10. Gichin Funakoshi, *Karate-do: My Way of Life* (Tokyo: Kodansha International, 1975), p. 38.

11. *Ibid.,* p. 42.

12. Robin L. Rielly, *The History of American Karate* (Little Ferry, N. J.: Semper-Fi Co., 1970).

CHAPTER 2

1. Hiroshi Kitagawa and Bruce T. Tsuchida, trans., *The Tale of the Heike: Heike Monogatari* (Tokyo: University of Tokyo Press, 1975), pp. 672–73.

2. Kenzo Akiyama, *The History of Nippon,* trans. Toshiro Shimanouchi (Tokyo: Kokusai Bunka Shinkokai, 1941), p. 150.

3. Kanichi Asakawa, ed., *The Documents of Iriki* (New Haven: Yale University Press, 1929).

4. Yanosuke Nakazato, "Japanese National Traits and Kendo, or Japanese Fencing," *Japan Illustrated 1934* (Tokyo), p. 918.

5. Inazo Nitobe, *Bushido: The Soul of Japan* (1905; reprint ed., Rutland and Tokyo: Charles E. Tuttle Co., 1969), p. 12.

6. Asakawa, *The Documents of Iriki,* p. 53.

7. Nitobe, *Bushido,* p. 163.

8. John W. Dower, ed., *Origins of the Modern Japanese State: Selected Writings of E. H. Norman* (New York: Pantheon Books, 1975), p. 360.

9. Carl Steenstrup, "The Imagawa Letter," *Monumenta Nipponica* XXVIII, no. 3 (1973), pp. 299–300.

10. Walter Dening, *Japan in Days of Yore* (Tokyo: Methodist Publishing House, 1906), pp. 157–59.

11. Wm. Theodore de Bary, ed., *Sources of Japanese Tradition* (New York: Columbia University Press, 1958), pp. 335–38.

12. *Ibid.,* p. 400.

13. Michiko Y. Aoki and Margaret B. Dardess, "The Popularization of Samurai Values: A Sermon by Hosoi Heishu," *Monumenta Nipponica* XXXI, no. 4 (1976), p. 393.

14. Roger F. Hackett, "Nishi Amane: A Tokugawa–Meiji Bureaucrat," *Journal of Asian Studies* XVIII, no. 2 (February 1969), p. 221.

15. de Bary, *Sources of Japanese Tradition,* p. 706.

16. Nitobe, *Bushido,* pp. 163–64.

17. Frank Brinkley, *Japan: Its History, Arts and Literature,* vol. II, (Boston: J. B. Millet Co., 1902), p. 173.

18. Max Weber, *The Sociology of Religion,* trans. Ephriam Fischoff (Boston: Beacon Press, 1963), pp. 171–76.

19. Takuan, "Fudochi Shinmyo Roku," trans. Mariko Akashi and Tad Tohan, *Traditions* I, no. 1 (1976), p. 16.

20. Miyamoto Musashi, *A Book of Five Rings: A Guide to Strategy,* trans. Victor Harris (Woodstock, N. Y.: Overlook Press, 1974), p. 95.

21. Eugen Herrigel, *Zen in the Art of Archery,* trans. R. F. C. Hull (New York: Vintage Books, 1971).

CHAPTER 3

1. For a more detailed account of a seppuku ritual, see A. B. Mitford, ed. *Tales of Old Japan* (1871; reprint ed., Rutland and Tokyo; Charles E. Tuttle Co., 1966), pp. 375–409.

2. Nobushige Amenomori, "War and the Japanese Woman," unpublished article [c. 1905] in the Griffis Collection, Series II, Box 8, Rutgers University, New Brunswick, N. J.

3. Ray A. Moore, "Adoption and Samurai Mobility in Tokugawa Japan," *Journal of Asian Studies* XXIX, no. 3 (May 1970), p. 621.

4. George Sansom, *Japan: A Short Cultural History* (New York: Appleton–Century–Croft, 1962), pp. 362–65.

CHAPTER 4

1. For a further discussion of these terms, see Joseph R. Levenson, *Confucian China and Its Modern Fate* (Berkeley: University of California Press, 1958), p. xiii–xix.

CHAPTER 7

1. Some of the older methods of practicing the forms along with their names may be found in Kanken Toyama, *Karate-Do Daihokan* (Tokyo: Tsuru Shobo, 1963).

2. Gichin Funakoshi, *Karate-do Kyohan,* trans. Tsutomu Oshima (Tokyo: Kodansha International, 1973), pp. 8–9.

APPENDIX

1. *International Shotokan Karate Federation Contest Rules* (Philadelphia: International Shotokan Karate Federation, 1979).

Selective Bibliography

RECOMMENDED READING

The books in the following annotated list of works in English have been selected to give the Western reader an insight into Japanese culture with a view toward understanding the traditions of the martial arts in Japan. It contains the works of contemporary and past martial arts practitioners and observers, as well as some basic books that discuss the history and culture of Japan and provide valuable background material for an understanding of the martial tradition.

Draeger, Donn F. and Smith, Robert W. *Comprehensive Asian Fighting Arts* (formerly *Asian Fighting Arts*). Tokyo: Kodansha International, 1969.
    In this work Draeger and Smith, both long-time practitioners of the combative arts and scholars in the field, trace the historic and contemporary development of the classic fighting arts of the Orient. Coverage includes kyujutsu (archery), *t'ai chi ch'uan,* and kendo, as well as descriptions of lesser-known arts practiced in India, Pakistan, Thailand, Malaysia, Indonesia, and the Philippines.

Funakoshi, Gichin. *Karate-do Kyohan.* Translated by Tsutomu Oshima. Tokyo: Kodansha International, 1973.
    Master Funakoshi, the first of the great karate masters who came from Okinawa to Japan proper to spread the art, first published this work in Japanese in 1936. The development and philosophy of karate and its techniques are discussed, and the original forms for all the kata of the Shotokan system are portrayed. The translator was a student of the master and is himself an expert in the Shotokan system.

Gluck, Jay. *Zen Combat,* New York: Ballantine Books, 1962.
    This is one of the early works published in the United States about the Japanese martial arts. Gluck's firsthand accounts of events surrounding Masatatsu Oyama and Gogen Yamaguchi make for fascinating reading. In addition, he discusses other arts, such as archery and aikido.

Haines, Bruce A. *Karate's History and Traditions.* Rutland and Tokyo: Charles E. Tuttle Co., 1968.
    Haine's book is a definitive history of the empty-hand combative arts known collectively as karate. Focusing on China, Japan, and Okinawa, Haines pieces together the history of karate, relying heavily on oral tradition, and using what little written material exists. There is a further section on the introduction of the art to Hawaii.

Harrison, E. J. *The Fighting Spirit of Japan*. 1912. Reprint. London: Foulsham & Co. 1976.

Harrison is a practitioner of judo, having spent a number of years in Japan prior to World War II. He outlines the development and practice of judo and karate and discusses some of the famous masters of the arts along with the Zen influence on them. Since Harrison was one of the first Westerners to become expert in a Japanese martial art, his work is particularly valuable in that he viewed the arts in their original form, before they became "Westernized."

Herrigel, Eugen. *Zen in the Art of Archery*. Translated by R. F. C. Hull. New York: Vintage Books, 1971.

Herrigel was a German professor of philosophy who went to Japan in the early 1940s to teach at a university there. He was fascinated by kyujutsu (archery) and became an avid practitioner. In this book he relates his experiences in training and how he perceived the influence of Zen on the art.

Miyamoto, Musashi. *A Book of Five Rings: A Guide to Strategy*. Translated by Victor Harris. Woodstock, N. Y.: Overlook Press, 1974.

For the Japanese who study the art of the sword, this work tops the list. It is also considered to be one of the basic books for anyone aspiring to mastery of any martial art. Written in the seventeenth century by a famous swordsman, it is really a philosophy book on how to master technique. Also included with this translation are a brief biography of the author's life and a description of Japanese society at the time of writing.

Nicol, C. W. *Moving Zen*. New York: William Morrow & Co., 1975.

Nicol is one of those recent visitors to Japan who took up the art of karate. He describes training at the headquarters of the Japan Karate Association and his experiences with some of the better-known JKA masters. This work is valuable in that it provides the reader with firsthand information on what it is like to train in Japan.

Nitobe, Inazo. *Bushido: The Soul of Japan*. 1905. Reprint. Rutland and Tokyo: Charles E. Tuttle Co., 1969.

Originally published in Japanese in 1899, Nitobe's book has become a classic on the subject of bushido, the code of the warrior. The work is a valuable guide to understanding Japanese culture; however, readers should be aware that it was written by an academic statesman who was not a practitioner of the martial arts.

Sansom, George. *A History of Japan*. 3 vols. Stanford: Stanford University Press, 1958–63.

For those wishing a detailed account of the history of Japan from its earliest records to 1867, these three volumes are probably the most complete available. Volume I (to 1334) covers the origins of the Japanese people, the early attempts to gain control over the islands, the introduction of Chinese culture, and the development of the samurai. Volume II (1334–1615) discusses Japan's feudal period and the struggle for power that resulted in the unification of Japan under the Tokugawa shogunate. Volume III (1615–1867) concerns the Tokugawa rule, relations with the West, internal developments, and the beginnings of modern Japan up to the Meiji Restoration.

Sansom, George. *Japan: A Short Cultural History*. Rev. ed. Stanford: Stanford University Press, 1952.

In this work Sansom discusses in detail the religions, class structure, arts, and basic political and societal developments of Japan. Valuable insights into the culture of the Japanese are provided. (The edition used by the author and included in the Notes —that of Appleton–Century–Croft—is now out of print.)

Shioya, Sakae. *Chushingura: An Exposition*. Tokyo: Hokuseido Press, 1956.

Those interested in Japanese martial arts may have heard references to the "tale of the 47 Ronin." The *Chushingura* is an eighteenth-century play by Takeda Izumo based on the original incident. In the present work the author relates in detail the history surrounding the incident and then follows with a full version of the play.

Takuan. "Fudochi Shinmyo Roku." Translated by Mariko Akashi and Tad Tohan. *Traditions* I, no. 1 (1976), pp. 9–34.

The role of Zen in the martial arts is explained in this letter of Takuan, a seventeenth-century Zen master, to the noted fencing expert, Yagyu Munenori. It is practical advice, designed to explain to the swordsman how to cast aside worldly concerns and maximize his training. For those interested in learning just what the connection between Zen and the martial arts is, this is probably the easiest explanation to understand.

Urban, Peter. *The Karate Dojo*. Rutland and Tokyo: Charles E. Tuttle Co., 1967.

Urban was the first man to bring Japanese Goju karate to America, having studied in Japan under Master Gogen Yamaguchi. His book is a collection of accounts of his observations of karate training in Japan and tales of famous karate masters and their teaching methods. In all, Urban's book provides valuable insights into the training in Japan from a Western point of view.

Yamamoto, Tsunetomo. *Hagakure: The Book of the Samurai*. Translated by William Scott Wilson. Tokyo: Kodansha International, 1979.

The *Hagakure*, originally written in 1716, is a collection of advisory comments of Yamamoto Tsunetomo, as recorded posthumously by his student Tsuramoto Tashiro. Yamamoto describes in detail what he perceives the samurai's role in society to be, illustrating his point with stories of events of the times and how they typify the samurai ideal. The *Hagakure* has long been regarded by Japanese scholars as one of the essential works for understanding the traditions of the samurai class.

REFERENCES IN ENGLISH

Akiyama, Kenzo. *The History of Nippon*. Translated by Toshiro Shimanouchi. Tokyo: Kokusai Bunka Shinkokai, 1941.

Aoki, Michiko Y. and Dardess, Margaret B. "The Popularization of Samurai Values: A Sermon by Hosoi Heishu." *Monumenta Nipponica* XXXI, no. 4 (1976), pp. 393–413.

Anesaki, Masaharu. *History of Japanese Religion*. London: Kegan Paul, Trench, Trubner & Co., 1930.

Asakawa, Kanichi, ed. *The Documents of Iriki.* New Haven: Yale University Press, 1929.

Beasley, W. G. *The Meiji Restoration.* Stanford: Stanford University Press, 1972.

————. *The Modern History of Japan.* New York: Praeger Publishers, 1963.

Bellah, Robert N. *Tokugawa Religion.* Glencoe, Ill.: Free Press, 1957.

Borton, Hugh. *Japan's Modern Century.* New York: Ronald Press Co., 1955.

Brinkley, Frank. *Japan: Its History, Arts and Literature.* Vol. II. Boston: J. B. Millet Co., 1902.

Bull, Earl R. *Ryuku: The Floating Dragon.* Newark, Ohio: Earl R. Bull, 1958.

Collcutt, Martin. *Five Mountains: The Rinzai Monastic Institution in Medieval Japan.* Cambridge: Harvard University Press, 1981.

Craig, Albert M. *Choshu in the Meiji Restoration.* Cambridge: Harvard University Press, 1961.

de Bary, Wm. Theodore, ed. *Sources of Japanese Tradition.* New York: Columbia University Press, 1958.

Dore, R. P. *Education in Tokugawa Japan.* Berkeley: University of California Press, 1965.

Dower, John W., ed. *Origins of the Modern Japanese State: Selected Writing of E. H. Norman.* New York: Pantheon Books, 1975.

Duus, Peter. *Feudalism in Japan.* New York: Alfred A. Knopf, 1976.

Egami, Shigeru. *The Heart of Karate-do* (formerly *The Way of Karate: Beyond Technique*). Tokyo: Kodansha International, 1976.

Fairbank, John K.; Reischauer, Edwin O.; and Craig, Albert M. *East Asia: The Modern Transformation.* Boston: Houghton Mifflin Co., 1965.

Flaceliere, Robert. *Daily Life in Greece.* New York: Macmillan Co., 1965.

Funakoshi, Gichin. *Karate-do: My Way of Life.* Tokyo: Kodansha International, 1975.

Gardiner, E. Norman. *Athletics of the Ancient World.* London: Oxford University Press, 1967.

Griffis, William Elliot. *The Mikado's Empire.* New York: Harper & Brothers, 1876.

————. *The Religions of Japan.* New York: Charles Scribner's Sons, 1895.

Hackett, Roger F. *Yamagata Aritomo in the Rise of Modern Japan.* Cambridge: Harvard University Press, 1971.

Hall, John W. and Jansen, Marius B., eds. *Studies in the Institutional History of Early Modern Japan.* Princeton: Princeton University Press, 1968.

Hall, John W. and Mass, Jeffrey P. *Medieval Japan.* New Haven: Yale University Press, 1974.

Harada, Tasuku. *The Faith of Japan.* New York: Macmillan Co., 1914.

Harootunian, Harry D. "The Economic Rehabilitation of the Samurai in the Early Meiji Period." *Journal of Asian Studies* XIX, no. 4 (August 1960), pp. 433–44.

Hoffman, Yoel, trans. *The Sound of the One Hand: Two Hundred Eighty-one Zen Koans and Answers.* New York: Basic Books, 1977.

Hoover, Thomas. *Zen Culture.* New York: Random House, 1977.

International Shotokan Karate Federation Contest Rules. Philadelphia: International Shotokan Karate Federation, 1979.

Jansen, Marius B., ed. *Changing Japanese Attitudes Toward Modernization.* Princeton: Princeton University Press, 1965.

————. *Sakamoto Ryoma and the Meiji Restoration.* Princeton: Princeton University Press, 1961.

Kaigo Tokiomi. *Japanese Education: Its Past and Present.* Tokyo: Kokusai Bunka Shinkokai, 1968.

Keenleyside, Hugh L. and Thomas, A. F. *History of Japanese Education and Present Educational System.* Tokyo: Hokuseido Press, 1937.

Kerr, George H. *Okinawa: The History of an Island People.* Rutland and Tokyo: Charles E. Tuttle Co., 1958.

Kikuchi, Komei. "The Way of the Bow." *The East,* October 1978, pp. 23–32.

Kim, Richard. *The Weaponless Warriors.* Burbank, Calif.: Ohara Publications, 1974.

Kitagawa, Hiroshi and Tsuchida, Bruce T., trans. *The Tale of Heike: Heike Monogatari.* Tokyo: University of Tokyo Press, 1975.

Levenson, Joseph R. *Confucian China and Its Modern Fate.* Berkeley: University of California Press, 1958.

Marshall, Byron. *Capitalism and Nationalism in Prewar Japan.* Stanford: Stanford University Press, 1967.

Mass, Jeffrey P. *Warrior Government in Early Medieval Japan.* New Haven: Yale University Press, 1974.

"Master Nakayama and the Long Journey of Karate." *The East,* August 1979, pp. 53–58.

Mitford, A. B. *Tales of Old Japan.* 2 vols. 1871. Reprint (2 vols. in 1). Rutland and Tokyo: Charles E. Tuttle Co., 1966.

Moore, Ray A. "Adoption and Samurai Mobility in Tokugawa Japan." *Journal of Asian Studies* XXIX, no. 3 (May 1970), pp. 617–32.

Motobu, Choki. *Okinawa Kempo: Karate-Jutsu on Kumite.* Olathe, Kan.: Ryukyu Imports, 1977.

Nagamine, Shoshin. *The Essence of Okinawan Karate-Do.* Rutland and Tokyo: Charles E. Tuttle Co., 1976.

Nakane, Chie. *Japanese Society.* Berkeley: University of California Press, 1970.

Nakazato, Yanosuke. "Japanese National Traits and Kendo, or Japanese Fencing." *Japan Illustrated 1934.* Tokyo.

New Brunswick, N. J.: Rutgers University. The Griffis Collection. Series II, Box 8. "War and the Japanese Woman" [by Nobushige Amenomori]. *c.* 1905.

Nishiyama, Hidetaka and Brown, Richard C. *Karate: The Art of "Empty-Hand" Fighting.* Rutland and Tokyo: Charles E. Tuttle Co., 1959.

Norman, E. Herbert. *Soldier and Peasant in Japan: The Origins of Conscription.* Vancouver: University of British Columbia, 1965.

Onishi, Eizo. *Right Karate-Do.* Mimeographed. Kanagawa, Japan, 1964.

Plato. *The Laws*. Translated by A. E. Taylor. New York: E. P. Dutton, 1960.

Quennell, Marjorie and Quennell, C. H. B. *Everyday Things in Ancient Greece*. Rev. ed. Edited by Kathleen Freeman. New York: G. P. Putnam's Sons, 1968.

Reischauer, Edwin O. and Fairbank, John K. *East Asia: The Great Tradition*. Boston: Houghton Mifflin Co., 1958.

Rielly, Robin L. *The History of American Karate*. Little Ferry, N. J.: Semper-Fi Co., 1970.

Sasamori, Junzo and Warner, Gordon. *This Is Kendo*. Rutland and Tokyo: Charles E. Tuttle Co., 1964.

Shinoda, Minoru. *The Founding of the Kamakura Shogunate*. New York: Columbia University Press, 1960.

Silberman, Bernard S. "Bureaucratization of the Meiji State: The Problem of Succession in the Meiji Restoration, 1868–1900." *Journal of Asian Studies* XXV, no. 3 (May 1976), pp. 421–30.

Singer, Kurt. *Mirror, Sword and Jewel*. New York: George Braziller, 1973.

Smethurst, Richard J. *A Social Basis for Prewar Japanese Militarism*. Berkeley: University of California Press, 1974.

Smith, Thomas C. *The Agrarian Origins of Modern Japan*. Stanford: Stanford University Press, 1959.

Steenstrup, Carl. "The Imagawa Letter," *Monumenta Nipponica* XXVIII, no. 3 (1973), pp. 295–316.

Suzuki, Daisetz T. *The Zen Doctrine of No-Mind*. London: Rider & Co., 1949.

———. *Zen Buddhism*. Edited by William Barrett. Garden City, N. Y.: Doubleday & Co., 1956.

"Takasebune." Translated by Tadashi Kikuoka. *Traditions* III, no. 1 (1979), pp. 7–21.

Turnbull, S. R. *The Samurai: A Military History*. New York: Macmillan Co., 1977.

Weber, Max. *The Sociology of Religion*. Translated by Ephriam Fischoff. Boston: Beacon Press, 1963.

REFERENCES IN JAPANESE

Mabuni, Ken'ei. *Karate-Do Kyohan*. Tokyo: Meiryudo, 1978.

Nakayama, Masatoshi. *Karate-Do Shinkyotei*. Tokyo: Tsuru Shobo, (no date).

Oya, Reikichi. *Karate no Narai Kata*. Tokyo: Kinensha, 1958.

Oyama, Masatatsu. *Waga Karate Gorin no Sho*. Tokyo: Kodansha, 1955.

Shukumine, Seiken. *Karate Tanren Sanka Getsu*. Tokyo: Nihon Bungeisha, 1980.

———. *Shin Karate-Do Kyohan*. Tokyo: Nihon Bungeisha, 1974.

Toyama, Kanken. *Karate-Do*. Tokyo: Tsuru Shobo, 1962.

———. *Karate-Do Nyumon*. Tokyo: Gembunsha, 1963.

———. *Karate-Do Daihokan*. Tokyo: Tsuru Shobo, 1963.

Yamazaki, Terutomo. *Mushin no Kokoro*. Tokyo: Supotsu Raifusha, 1980.

Index